The Second Bailout:

A Personal Memoir of Bombing Missions over Nazi Germany and Life as a POW

Weldon D. Squyres
as told to Cynthia S. Price

Edited by Cynthia S. Price

PublishAmerica
Baltimore

First printing

ISBN: 1-4137-1129-4
PUBLISHED BY PUBLISHAMERICA, LLLP
www.publishamerica.com
Baltimore

Printed in the United States of America

Dedicated to the men and women, civilians and military personnel, who served in World War II. You changed the course of history, making the world a better place for my generation and future generations. Thank you.

C. S. P.

And Vietnam!

Thanks, Vet!

Cynthia S. Price

This book would not have been completed without the support, help and encouragement of my beloved husband, Marty Price, whom I met while working in the Space Program in Houston; and without the assistance of my cousin, Dallas Lee Squyres, the firstborn son of Weldon Squyres. Lee was the first to make his father's story known to the rest of our family. We now share it with you.

TABLE OF CONTENTS

FOREWORD

Even though war veterans may share many experiences, it seems that ultimately many of them may tend to have their own unique, personal recollections of events.

His family got the impression that Weldon Squyres, a World War II bomber crewman who became a German prisoner, didn't want to talk about his wartime experiences. So they didn't bring up the subject.

But fortunately, in later years when his niece, Cynthia S. Price, became curious about his military service and broached the subject with him, he then was very willing to share his memories with frankness and humor and offer his personal perceptions.

In the course of a long correspondence with Price, Squyres vividly and movingly recalled his military service and his brushes with death as a bomber crewman in the final stages of the war when the Germans moved the prisoners from his camp before advancing Allied forces could liberate them.

In the course of a long, lively correspondence, Squyres vividly recalled his military service and brushes with death when on two occasions B-24 Liberator bombers he was serving on were shot down. He evaded capture the first time but not the second time.

Price would assist him in getting the prisoner of war medal he had earned. It is regrettable he didn't live to see this book.

Bob Tutt
Houston Chronicle Military History Writer
Houston, Texas

INTRODUCTION

There comes a time in most people's lives when they begin to see family members only at funerals. People grow older, marry, have children and then hectic lives, move away, and lose touch with aunts, uncles and cousins. Before you know it, years and even decades pass before you see again the favorite relatives you remember and liked so much when you were a child.

Too many times when you see them again, it is too late. These were my thoughts in January 1988 when I was attending the funeral of my aunt, Wanda Squyres, in Lubbock, Texas.

She was Aunt Sug ("Shug"—short for "Sugar") to my brothers, sister, cousins, and me, Cynthia Squyres Price. I remember her as a beautiful, dainty, fashionable southern lady. She was the only girl in her family—her brothers being my father, Tom Squyres (family name "Lec"), and my uncle, Weldon Squyres, whom we occasionally called Skip. I remembered thinking at the time of her funeral that I was getting tired of dutifully returning to Lubbock to attend painful family funerals.

But there was a bright spot to this particular trip. My Uncle Weldon, whom I had lost contact with over the years, was there. He was one of my favorite relatives because he was the father of some of my favorite cousins!

Weldon had five children—four boys and one girl—our "California cousins" as my brothers, sister and I called them when we were growing up in Texas. Three of his kids paired up, in terms of age, to the four kids in my family. His oldest child, Lee, was about the same age as my oldest brother, Tom. Weldon's next son, Drew, was about my brother Jerry's age. Brian was closest in age to my sister Becky and me (we were born 13 months apart). Weldon's two

13

smallest children, Margaret and Paul, were younger than the rest of us, so we didn't hang out much together as cousins, or as kids, when we were growing up.

At Sug's funeral, Weldon and I had another chance to renew our uncle-niece relationship. We talked extensively, and as fate would have it, we found we had much in common—a mutual love for fishing, boating, and travels to Mexico.

Weldon told me that in the next few weeks he was moving from his California Bay Area home without his wife, Nikki, (for reasons I never knew nor asked about) to relocate to Santiago—a small town near the Pacific coast city of Manzanillo, Mexico. He thought that I would have never heard of Santiago—it being so small and not a mecca for American tourists. But I surprised him when I told him that not only had I heard of Santiago, I had been there only a few weeks before!

I had pleasant memories of Santiago, which I shared with my Uncle Weldon. He promised that when he moved to Santiago in the next few weeks, he would write me and we would continue our conversations about our favorite subjects. Plus, I promised to introduce him to my hobbies of birdwatching and deep-sea fishing, if only by letter.

Through our letters, we discovered that we both wanted to be writers. It was his ambition in his younger days—to travel and write. He majored in Journalism at Texas Tech University in 1941 before joining the armed forces a year and a half later. (He later wrote me in his war account: "Well, the travel transpired, but the writing fell by the wayside.") At the time of our correspondence, I was returning to college to take writing courses in an attempt to become a professional writer. His letters also served to encourage my writing.

At the funeral, I didn't tell him but there was something else I wanted to talk about with him. I had been told since my childhood never to bring up this subject—Weldon had been a prisoner of war held by the Nazis during World War II. His having been a POW was a taboo subject in my family.

The forbidden subject had surfaced for me before the funeral, when I learned that the U.S. Government now had a POW medal. I wondered if my uncle would receive one. I wondered if he wanted one.

I raised the subject during a visit by my dad sometime after the funeral. To my great surprise Dad said, "You ought to ask Weldon about his POW experiences. He'll be happy to tell you all about it."

After Dad's visit, I called my sister. "Do I remember correctly that we weren't ever to bring up that subject?" I asked her.

"That's what I remember," she said. My curiosity was now piqued more than ever.

Shortly after the time my uncle Weldon moved to Santiago and we began to write each other, I broached the subject to him in a letter. My dad was right—Weldon was happy to tell me about his war and POW experiences. He explained that he never told anybody because no one ever asked about it. He just figured it was "ancient history" to my generation. ("…I have forgotten many of the details. Of course, I remember the constant terror and fear of not living through it…") But I told him we never asked because we were told not to. I had also confirmed this with my cousin Lee.

The result of my casual inquiry was his story told to me in engaging and extraordinary letters—a story that had not been previously told and in fact forbidden to most of the family. Now I am pleased to share his unique wartime experiences.

World War II caused monumental changes in families. All the men of Weldon's family wanted to do their share. Weldon's brother (my father) joined the Army Air Corps and was accepted into flight training as a cadet. At age 47, Weldon's father (my grandfather) joined the Army Corps of Engineers and was sent to England to help build air bases there. The rest of the family, Weldon's mother (my grandmother) and his sister (Aunt Sug), moved from the small town of Fluvanna, Texas (population about 375 in 1940), to Lubbock to be closer to Weldon who at 17 was enrolled at Texas Tech University.

As soon as Weldon turned 18 and finished his current semester at Tech in January 1943, he joined the war effort. "I was the only 'man' in the family left and afraid that the war would be over before I was old enough to enlist…I listed [in preference] the Army Infantry, then the Marines, thinking either of those two would be the quickest paths to action." A bone depression in his chest made him fear that the military would not accept him. But he was assigned to the U.S. Army Air Corps (today's Air Force) for training as an aircraft radio operator/mechanic.

After basic training and gunnery school, he was assigned to a bomber crew on a B-24, "The Liberator." According to Weldon, "The B-17, the 'Flying Fortress,' got all the publicity during and after the war, but the 'Lib' was much faster, carried a heavier bomb load and had a longer range than the Fort."

Weldon was correct. The B-24 Liberator was produced in greater numbers and flown in war by more countries than any other four-engine bomber in WWII. Over 19,200 B-24s in several versions were manufactured between 1939 and 1945.

Even though the B-17 received most of the publicity, B-24s outnumbered the Flying Fortresses, even in the battles in Europe. At altitudes of up to 28,000 feet, it could also fly higher than the B-17 but alas, it was known as "The Box Car" almost as often as "The Liberator."

A combat-ready B-24 carried a crew of ten and when fully armed, weighed more than 60,000 pounds. The most common versions had four movable gun turrets, each with two .50 caliber machine guns and two .50s in the waist turret for a total of ten machine guns. Later versions had eleven. The usual bomb load was ten 500-pound bombs or five bombs of 1,000 pounds each.

The B-24 was powered by four 1,200 hp engines and carried 2,750 gallons of fuel. Many B-24 missions involved round trips of 1,500 to 2,000 miles. Over Europe, a standard mission altitude was from 18,000 to 28,000 feet, although some missions were flown much lower. The planes were not pressurized or heated, and temperatures could reach minus 30 deg. F and below.

A B-24 was a little over 66 feet in length, about 18 feet tall, with a wingspan of 110 feet and a maximum speed of slightly more than 300 mph. To the men who flew in her, she was a precision war machine, a lifeboat, or a flying casket.

After crew training in June 1944, Weldon was dispatched to Foggia in southern Italy to the 782nd Squadron, 465th Heavy Bomber Group, 15th Air Force. In almost 20 missions, he would fly to southern France, southern Germany, northern Italy, Yugoslavia and Romania. (The 15th Air Force began bombing operations in November 1943 and continued until April 1945 when a bombardment by 1,233 heavy bombers dropped nearly 25,000 bombs on German forces. Germany surrendered on May 7, 1945.)

Weldon became a radio operator/gunner on B-24s. He didn't know it, but he would be shot down and forced to jump out of planes twice. The first bailout was on his very first bombing run, a mission for which he volunteered, not telling anyone that he had not previously been in combat. He parachuted out of the badly damaged plane, landing in an Italian vineyard. He was returned quickly to his base where he learned that he was scheduled to fly a mission again the very next day.

His 19th mission (a tour of duty was 50 missions) began on August 3, 1944, and included the entire 782nd Squadron. The target was Nazi aircraft factories at Frederickshaefen, Germany. Over 600 heavy bombers were dispatched on this mission. Defensive fire was heavy and eleven B-24s were lost, including Weldon's. Two of his crewmembers were killed, but he and the other survivors bailed out. This was his second bailout and would lead to his becoming a prisoner of war.

Weldon and other downed airmen were soon captured and taken by train to an encampment at Garmish-Partenkirchen, a small city in the Alps. When he first saw the encampment, Weldon realized that he had seen this sight before in a nightmare he had had a few years earlier when he was boy.

After interrogation, Weldon was transferred in a boxcar to a POW camp (stalag) at St. Wendel in southern Germany's Saar Basin Valley near the French border. ("I later realized these were the same boxcars the Germans used to transport to their deaths in other stalags and concentration camps, the hapless Jews and other unfortunates who did not fit Hitler's Aryan mold.") About a month later (mid-September), he was moved again to Stalag Luft 6 outside the small village of Kiefheide in Nazi-occupied eastern Poland. During this transfer, Weldon and the other POWs endured a harrowing night of bombing by their own Allied planes.

Weldon was held at Stalag Luft 6 for the remainder of 1944. As the war turned against Germany's favor, conditions worsened in the POW camp. "I traded my senior high school class ring to a guard for a can full of sugar." In January 1945, he and the other POWs were forced on a march of 300 miles across frozen northern Germany. Two months later, he and two comrades would make their "escape" into another German POW camp, this one holding British prisoners. On April 16, 1945, the camp was liberated by the British 8th Army under General Bernard Law "Monty" Montgomery.

Weldon weighed 117 pounds. He and his American comrades were sent to a U.S. Army debarkation center wearing British Tommy uniforms with snazzy berets. While traveling by ship on the way home to the U.S., he received word of the German surrender. A month after his liberation, he arrived home at Lubbock, Texas.

During the course of his correspondence to me, I informed Weldon about the new POW medal. I obtained the official application and mailed it to him in Mexico. He submitted it and was found qualified to receive the medal. Because of the insecurity of the Mexican postal system, he instructed that it be mailed to his California home where it arrived in October 1989. But he would never see it. (Epilogue.)

This account of his war and POW experiences is told in his own words. For a young man from a small Texas town, World War II was an extraordinary experience. "To a naïve, idealistic, romantic 18-19 year-old-boy whose horizons were bounded by where he had lived in West Texas and by what he had read, this [war] was all pretty heady stuff…"

The war was an extraordinary experience for his entire generation. He wrote, "I think the U.S. was the most united in anger and purpose during those years than at any other time in its history, or since…the democracy of the armed forces had finally brought us all together and in no circumstances more intimately than in a POW camp. For me, it was an enlightening and educational experience."

Beginning with his more recent accounts of living in Mexico through the correspondence where I ask him about his life as a POW, we now share this enlightening and educational experience with you.

Cynthia S. Price

Chapter 1
Mexico
"Thank God beer is inexpensive, and you don't have to boil it!"

Manzanillo, Colima, Mexico
17 de Junio 1988 [June 17, 1988]

Dear Cindy,

I have been in Mexico about a month and a half now, and am pretty well settled in. I have a nice, large apartment right on the beach. It's only one bedroom (I couldn't find a two), but it's large, open and spacious, with plenty of room to make down beds. I intend to buy some portable, fold-up ones soon.

The walls are all whitewashed with red tile floors throughout. On the front I have a large covered veranda with the same red tile floor. Beyond that is the front yard, some grass but mostly sand, with several loaded coconut palms, an almond tree, and some others which I don't know. There is a low, stone retaining wall, and then—the Pacific Ocean!

Manzanillo is not a pretty town and is not a tourist town except for Mexicans who come to the beaches. You seldom see a *Norte Americano* [North American] in town. There are two enclaves further out of town, Las Hadas and Club Santiago, which cater to American tourists, but they are very expensive hotels and condominiums, which seem to draw the two-week vacationers and six-month snowbirds. For some reason they don't come into town much.

Manzanillo is an old city—ships from the Spanish fleet sailed out of this harbor in 1654 to conquer the Philippines. Its economy is supported by commercial fishing, ocean and rail shipping, mining, and local agriculture which produces an abundance of good fruits, melons and vegetables. The weather is hot and humid, but I almost always have a cooling breeze off the ocean.

I am about 9 kilometers from town, just about half-way between town and another little village, Santiago, where I sometimes go shopping. Most things are cheap, a six-pack of beer is $2.20 U.S., a liter of good vodka is $3.75. Food is cheap. I eat out a lot, a good shrimp dinner with a bottle of beer is around $5.00 and is usually more than I can eat. Other things are very expensive, even though made in Mexico. Pots and pans for the kitchen and furniture in general is very expensive. I paid about $25 for a plain old aluminum 2-liter tea kettle so I could boil water! Thank God beer is inexpensive, and you don't have to boil it!

I don't have a car yet, intend to get one next month when I have a C.D. which will mature, maybe a good used VW bug (which they still make here). The dealers won't finance a used car and the banks won't finance a *turista* [tourist], period, no matter how good your U.S. references may be. Anyway the interest rates are outrageous.

Meantime I have been doing very well with the buses. They run often, will stop almost anywhere and are cheap. It costs about 20 cents to go into either Manzanillo or Santiago. So far I have never seen another American on the bus. I used to draw some curious looks, but people seem to have gotten used to me now. Intercity bus and train fares are also very cheap compared to the U.S. I have even begun to wonder if I should get a car.

The people are very nice, friendly, and patient with my minimum Spanish. Evidently there is very little crime, and I can walk anywhere, anytime in Manzanillo and feel perfectly safe. I have seen only a few beggars (mostly disabled in some way) and there are no kids on the streets hustling you for a shoeshine or trying to peddle their sister.

I have some Berlitz tapes and workbooks and I am getting private tutoring twice a week (2 hours for $3.00 per hour), so my Spanish is improving some. I still slip into Portuguese, though. (Remember when I lived in Brazil for over two years?)

I have a maid three afternoons a week for $6.60 U.S. per week! My apartment is $152.00 per month! Can you believe it! When I left Santa Barbara, I was paying $750 per month for a little 2-bedroom apartment.

I want you guys to come to see me. Write, or give me a call. I'm sure you can dial direct. Country code for Mexico is 52, the area code here is 333, and my number is————. Just got my phone in yesterday, cost me $770 U.S.!

Let me know when you will be coming!

Love,
Your Unc

[Editor's note: Sadly, my response letter was not composed on my computer and so I do not have a copy of it. But I do remember telling my uncle about staying at a private villa in Manzanillo earlier in the year and going into Santiago to do some grocery shopping. The area is just as he describes: there are few Americans and the locals are very friendly. When my friend Shirley and I were in the grocery store in Santiago—a small non-air-conditioned establishment—we were the only Anglo *senoras* there. I remember a young mother with a new baby in her shopping cart, stopped and waved me to go in front of her with my cart. I looked at her baby girl and exclaimed "muy bonita!" (very beautiful!) much to her proud delight. A man I assumed to be the manager of the store bagged our groceries and carried them to our car with great formality and flourish.

Shirley told me that Santiago brags that 90% of the population is in church every Sunday morning. I believe it. I have never experienced so much genuine courtesy and hospitality to foreigners as I did in 1988 in the little Mexican town of Santiago. I hope Santiago never changes.]

Manzanillo, Colima, Mexico
17 de Agosto 1988 [August 17, 1988]

Dear Cindy Lou (I know you are Cynthia Anne, but Cindy Lou just always sounded so right to me!),

What a delight to get your nice letter and to find you have experienced Manzanillo and Santiago and like it as much as I do. What was the weather like in January? Right now we are in the rainy season, and the weather is hot and humid, very tropical. But yesterday there was a storm out to sea, and we had some fairly high winds and rain that has cooled things off nicely. It rained all night last night without let-up, and has been raining all morning, today, with still some very fresh breezes. The surf makes a continuous booming, rolling almost right up to the retaining wall of my front yard. I stood at the wall for awhile this morning in the rain, watching the surf. I love it.

Nikki [his wife, my aunt] came down the last week of July and the first week of August, and we had a great time. We stayed here a few days while I showed her the "sights," then decided to head for the mountains, to beat the heat, to see more of the country, and to try out the intercity transportation system. We took the train from here to Guadalajara, about a 7 hour trip with one stop in Colima (city, the capital of the state). We went first class, in a very comfortable, easy riding, air-conditioned coach, with wide plush seats and big "picture windows." They served us a large club sandwich with potato salad, a soft drink, and a dessert, all included in the whopping $7.50 fare! They also had a snack bar where you could buy juice, soft drinks, beer, and various munchies at nominal prices.

The country between here and Colima is very tropical, with huge coconut and banana plantations and occasional fields of sugarcane. Colima is in the foothills of the southern Sierra Madre range, and past Colima we climbed into wild beautiful mountain country with deep, steep canyons carrying rivers roaring from recent rains, and broad green valleys with cattle grazing, and occasional huge iron ore mining operations. And thus on into Guadalajara, in the early evening.

Guadalajara sits atop the high central plateau at a little over 5,200 ft. elevation. It is the second [populous] city in Mexico with population pushing close to 3 million. It is a beautiful modern, cosmopolitan city, with gorgeous plazas, parks, gardens, fountains and statuary. Nikki and I had spent a week's vacation there several years before, and we enjoyed re-visiting remembered sights. The weather was perfect—temperature in the mid-70s.

After a couple of days, we pushed on high into the mountains, this time by first class bus. We had made reservations and purchased tickets the day before, and picked the two front seats (assigned seating) to the right of the driver, so we had excellent views. We were bound for Guanajuato (pop. 80,000; elevation 6,724 ft.), one of the old colonial silver-mining cities that helped make Spain rich in the 1500s and 1600s. It also figured strongly in Mexico's later struggle for independence. In nearby Dolores Hidalgo, on 16 September 1810, a young Mexican priest, Father Miguel Hidalgo, first proclaimed independence from Spain. He was captured by Spanish troops in 1811, and his head, along with those of three other revolutionaries, adorned the four corners of the granary in Guanajuato, from 1811 until 1821, as a warning to other would-be revolutionaries. A very picturesque and charming old city. Again, the weather was perfect—low 70's.

On to San Miguel de Allende (pop. 16,000; elevation 6,134 ft.), a pretty little colonial town that has been declared a national monument. Over the years, it has become quite a renowned culture center, much like Taos, New Mexico, and has attracted a large colony of American ex-pats, mostly ex-teachers, writers, sculptors, artists, etc. Nothing spectacular, just a pretty little mountain city with cobblestone streets and enjoyable to wander around in. I saw more *gringos* in San Miguel in a day and a half than I have seen in 3-1/2 months here.

Not wanting to re-trace the same steps back to Guadalajara, we took a bus from San Miguel to Celaya, to the south toward Mexico

City, situated at the crossroads of two major highways, about 200 km from San Miguel. This was a second class bus, only one available, and the air conditioning was open windows with the wind blowing a gale. But the fare was a staggering 66 cents! At Celaya, we caught a better bus to Guadalajara, arriving there again early evening for a last night before catching the train next day for Manzanillo. It was a grand trip, and half the fun was finding our way around on our own, and it was incredibly cheap! I have decided against buying a car— getting around locally is no problem, and travel within the country is too easy and inexpensive to justify the capital investment, maintenance, insurance and gasoline costs.

Mi casa es su casa! Please come and visit. And I look forward to hearing from your friend Shirley. Maybe she will take me to one of the fancy bars in Las Hadas and buy me a drink!

Dear Cindy, please don't think I am being nosy, but I would like to hear more about your reunion, if you don't mind telling me about it. I always loved you four kids almost as if you were my own. I have been sorry that circumstances and time and distances have separated me from all of you these past several years. That's why I feel so great at re-establishing this communication with you after all these years. I love you, Dear Heart. Don't drift away again.

Well, enough of being somewhat maudlin! Write when you can, and let me know when you can come down.

Abrazos y Besos from your lovin' Unk

Chapter 2
Family
"My generation is beginning to look like the 'old folks' now."

Houston, Texas
September 6, 1988

Dear Weldon,

I received your August 17th letter last Saturday. I enjoyed reading about your train trip very much.

Since I last wrote you, I have quit my job as a legal secretary and started two classes in writing at the local college. I now have to use my computer at home, which isn't anywhere as nice as the one I had at work.

I've already told you about my friend, Shirley——. You may be hearing from her even before you receive this letter from me. She will probably be at the villa in Las Hadas some time before the end of September and definitely around October 29. She said she would call you and show you around Las Hadas, but *you* would have to buy the drinks!

Of course I don't think you're nosy asking about the reunion. I would have gone into more detail in my last letter, but I was so excited to reminisce about Manzanillo and Santiago with you. Last January when we were in Lubbock for Wanda's funeral, we said that it was a shame that it took a funeral to get everyone together. I talked to Becky [my sister] when I got back and I told her that I thought that she had better make plans to see the grandfolks *this year* before it was too late.

Then Becky and I came up with a plan to organize a family reunion in El Paso and get us four kids there and all our kids. The hardest part, of course, was to get everybody in El Paso, but everybody was there.

I am enclosing some pictures of the reunion to share with you. Please send these back to me, but if you want copies, let me know and I will have copies made for you.

I guess I am all out of news for now. Please keep in touch. I am enjoying your letters so much. Don't know when, but we would like to go back to Mexico to catch the sailfish that got away last time we were there!

Love,
Cindy

P. S. Did I ever tell you about my trip to Akumal on the Yucatan peninsula south of Cancun? It is a lovely, unknown, undeveloped, unspoiled place and one I would like to go to again before it is gone forever. I give it 10 years max before it is ruined by resorts and young American tourists.

Manzanillo, Colima, Mexico
Lunes, 3 de Ocubre 1988 [Monday, October 3, 1988]

Dear Cindy,

I had your letter (and pix) in the mailbox when I got home from Lubbock on the 15th of September. That was on a Thursday, and Friday the 16th is Mexico's independence day and everything was closed, so I didn't get the mail until Saturday. The P. O. is open till 1:00 on Saturdays. I was downtown most of the day on Friday enjoying the parades and festivities, all quite colorful.

Thanks for sharing your reunion news and pix with me, I enjoyed them very much. I am so glad that you were all able to get together, and from the pix, looked like you were having a good time. I wish you all could have come to your grandparents' reunion, we had a big crowd, must have been 60 to 70 people, and enough good food for twice that many. Mother and Dad, along with Mother's sisters Treacy and Bill (Dell Marie) and Aunt Ada (90 years old), and Mother's sister-in-law (widow of Uncle Barnie) are the only old-timers left. My generation of cousins is beginning to look like the "old folks" now, and there were 12 of us there. More and more the crowd is made up of your generation and their flocks and flocks of kids and in many cases, grandkids. And there are oodles of young children and babies, which is good—the family is thriving. I thoroughly enjoyed it, and Mother and Dad did too. I'm glad I went back, I don't think Mother could have managed with Dad and Aunt Treacy both, without me. I spent two weeks in Lubbock after the reunion, just to be with the folks and see how they are getting along. Considering their ages, they're doing great—both still active and able to do for themselves, but inevitably getting more feeble. I can see more changes each time I go back. Don't know how much longer they are going to make it, but they have had long, full lives, full of happiness and grief, as all lives are, but I think their experiences have made them grow, as they have coped with everything life has handed them. I am so thankful for the change in your father's attitude toward them—that has been a great blessing to them, and has lifted a great burden of sorrow and distress from their shoulders.

We have ignored some of each other's questions in our letters. I asked you how the weather was here in January? But I remember from your picture that you were wearing shorts, so I assume it must be pretty nice and dry. It's still raining off and on here, and the days are still hot and muggy. But the heat is abating somewhat, and the evenings and nights are quite pleasant. I can sleep now without the ceiling fan on in the bedroom.

My place is on the water which I love—the sound of the surf puts me to sleep each night.

There's not much news from here. My Spanish progress has sort of hit on a plateau—in fact it's sliding downhill. When Nikki was here the end of July/first of August, I discontinued my private tutoring sessions, then when she returned to California my tutor was on vacation through the rest of August. Then I left for Lubbock September 1 and have not resumed since my return.

I brought back so many books and other reading material, plus crossword puzzle books, etc. that I have not even been listening to my tapes and studying the workbooks. I've also been spending a lot of time with my computer chess game, boning up. I have had a few games downtown with some of the locals at my "local" bar, and found I am not in their league. So, what with reading, working x-word puzzles, playing chess, listening to baseball (and now football) games on the radio, I have sadly neglected my Spanish. But soon— my nose back on the grindstone!

Back to another of your questions—no, you have never told me about your trip to the Yucatan. Cindy, we haven't talked in years! Except briefly in Lubbock at Sug's funeral. Margaret [his daughter, my cousin] and her boyfriend spent a couple of weeks in the Yucatan last winter, also south of Cancun, and she was fascinated by it. I always have wanted to go, but have never been there. I'm tentatively planning a train trip there this winter. Meantime, tell me about your experiences.

Dear Heart, I've put a check mark on a couple of your pictures that

I would enjoy having copies of, but don't go to any trouble. It's the one of you four kids with your mother, and the one of all my grand nieces and nephews. Please write again all the names and ages on the back (the nieces and nephews. I know you four and Beth.)

Write when you have time. Tell me about the writing courses you are taking. What kind of writing and what for? Personal pleasure? Some kind of goal in mind? Incidentally, you write beautifully. I really enjoy your letters.

Your loving Unk,
Weldon

Houston, Texas
October 19, 1988

Dear Weldon,

As always, it is great to hear from you, whether on the phone or through the mail.

I remembered when I sealed my last letter to you that you had inquired about the weather there in January, and I forgot to tell you. They said it was 92 degrees and it must have been dry because I got cold coming out of the pool. The bougainvillea were in full bloom and there was a gardener at the villa every day watering, so it must have been the dry season. I bought a bougainvillea in March and it has started blooming now with our cooler weather. Are the bougainvillea still in bloom there? Do they bloom all year round there? I also bought a hibiscus for my patio since our trip because of the many flowers there.

I will get copies of those pictures made for you.

My brother Tom, his wife, and girl, Leslie, were here two weekends ago. We spent Saturday at NASA's Johnson Space Center here in Houston and Sunday at the big airshow that has the Confederate Air Force. We had a big time. I told them that I like going to the airshow every year because with each passing year it is less likely the old warbirds will keep flying. Sure enough, the following weekend at an airshow in Harlingen, the A-20 Havoc bomber—the only flying one left—crashed, killing the pilot. Apparently there was nothing wrong with the plane. The pilot had a heart attack and lost control. I would love to get Dad to come to one of these airshows. I think he would love it. Last year I made a video tape of the airshow and will send him a copy of it for Christmas. I don't suppose you have a VCR in Mexico, huh?

About Yucatan. We stayed at Akumal, about 60 miles south of Cancun. We flew into Cancun and rented an old VW car with no air conditioning (it doesn't exist in Mexico) and a cracked windshield. We packed our luggage and ourselves into it and drove at breakneck speed, dodging trucks and busses, down the highway to Akumal. As I wrote earlier, it is still relatively unspoiled. It is built around a small lagoon protected by a reef. The beaches are of white sand and coconut trees. The water of the Caribbean looks unreal at first with its aqua and green colors. To me it looked so unreal, like a big American producer was making a movie and had the water artificially colored for special effects. We spent most of four days snorkeling in the shallow lagoon. We hired an open boat and went bottom fishing in the Caribbean and caught some lovely red grouper. The water is so clear you can see the bright red fish way down in the water as you are pulling the line up. Our *capitan* would jump over the side of the boat into the water and catch live bait with his hands. After fishing, he took us to an uninhabited lagoon where a Mayan ruin jutted out in the water. We snorkeled there while he tried to catch lobster and an octopus for the restaurant. It was like watching a pearl diver. We really felt like Robinson Crusoe at times. We spent a day at Tulum to see the large Mayan ruins. There are ruins all over the peninsula. The whole Yucatan is ruined (bad joke). As you're driving down the highway, you can see thatched huts built on top of ruins.

The couple we were with had been there about two years before. They noticed that many of the farms had been abandoned in the two years that they were last there. We theorized that the locals are leaving their farms and getting jobs at the many resorts that are springing up all over the coast.

I wonder what kind of damage Hurricane Gilbert did to the reefs. I noticed when I was snorkeling that if I stood on a reef or pushed off with my flippers, it scarred the reef. They are that delicate. I also got stung on the knee by a small anemone. (While at the villa, I got bit by a small iguana. I never did learn to keep my hands off the local flora and fauna!)

We saw two water spouts form while staying at Yucatan and experienced one of the frequent blackouts. After a customary late dinner, we were walking from the restaurant across the beach back to our rooms when we saw the lights blink out all up and down the peninsula. We actually had to grope to find our rooms and read the room numbers by touch!

What I would like to do in Yucatan is rent a car (or take a train trip) and go to Merida. Also tour all the Mayan ruins. I love the black beans and honey that they serve for every meal, including breakfast. The Yucatan people seem to be more short and stout. It seems to me I see their Mayan heritage in them. I read a couple of books about the Mayans and the ruins so I would know what to look for when I saw some ruins. We also saw a few large bee hives in the jungle and I wondered if they were killer bees. They say Texas will have killer bees in a couple of years. I heard they are quite prominent in the Yucatan.

If you go to Yucatan, please tell me of your visit. You will see long, hanging bird nests. Those are from the oropendola. I saw many nests, but no birds. I have a bird book on Mexican birds. Those black parrot-like birds you see in Manzanillo are called ani.

You asked about my writing. I am taking composition and creative writing because I want to write. My teacher says that true writers say they want to write, not that they want to be writers. I am also doing some freelance work for a local advertising agency. I wrote a speech for a female aerospace executive and I also wrote some ad copy, newspaper announcement and press release for a Woman of the Year award.

I would really like to write science fiction in the same vein as Robert A. Heinlein. He is my favorite author. He died last May. Several people in the Houston area tried to persuade NASA to name the space station after him. I called and talked to a NASA official in Washington myself, but to no avail. It was Heinlein's death that made me quit my job at the law office and take the plunge to see if I could write.

Mostly, I like writing to my interesting relatives!

[And then I gently asked the question that had been burning in my mind for several years.]

Let me ask you something if I may. Since we were little, the kids in our family knew that you were a POW in Germany in WWII, but we somehow got the impression that we weren't to mention it or talk to you about it. I remember when the program "Hogan's Heroes" first came on TV. Mom said she didn't find it funny. She thought it was offensive and reminded us that our Uncle Skip had been a POW. A few years ago, Dad was visiting me and I asked him about it. He surprised me by saying that I could ask you about your experiences, that you would be glad to tell me about it. I asked Becky if she recalled that we were told not to mention it or ask about it and she said that's what she remembered. All I know is that you were a POW in Germany for the last few months of WWII. If you would like, I would very much like to know about it. That is, only if you want to write me about it.

Please let me hear from you when you get the chance.

Your loving niece,
Cindy

Chapter 3
The War Saga Begins
"I have no more problems talking about my stint as a POW...
I remember the constant terror and fear of not living through it..."

Domingo, 6 de Noviembre 1988 [Sunday, November 6, 1988]
Manzanillo, Colima, Mexico

Dear Cindy Lou,

How nice it is to get your wonderful letters! You write so
beautifully—you *are* a writer. Oddly enough, that was my ambition
in my younger days. I wanted to travel and write. Well, the travel
transpired, but the writing fell by the wayside. A buddy of mine in
high school was a good amateur photographer and we wanted to
travel, write and take pictures for *National Geographic*. We (I) even
wrote a letter to the *N.G.* editor outlining our ambitions (without
revealing that we were juniors in high school!), and had a nice reply,
asking for samples of our work—which of course we had nothing
worth submitting except some high school English themes, and some
pretty good pictures that Dick had taken on the family (Miller) ranch.
So that dream went a glimmering. Incidentally, Dick Miller has lived
in Spain for the past 25-30 years, and has become quite a renowned
artist. I went on to Texas Tech [Lubbock] in the fall of 1941 as a
Journalism major, and continued for 1-1/2 years until I went into the
service where I went to radio school and became interested in
electronics.

After the war I continued my studies in Communications
Electronics, and as you probably remember, was in the radio and

television broadcast industry for the rest of my working career, first on the engineering side, later into international marketing. The kind of writing I had to do, technical and marketing reports, etc., was pretty prosaic, and tended to stifle whatever "creativity" I might once have had. I did however, from time to time, write some pretty awful poetry, which I always threw away. So—I am glad there is a "writer" in the family!

I discovered last Sunday (a week ago) that my phone had been out of service for a week! So I never did hear from your friend Shirley. I never received my first (July) bill, so of course never paid it, thinking that when I paid my August bill it would naturally include any arrears. Not so. Each month's bill is separate and apart to itself! They cannot be co-mingled! So, I paid my September bill thinking all was current, but toward the end of October I began to wonder why I hadn't had any phone calls for awhile. (Mother usually calls once a week.) So I picked up the phone—dead. I went to the phone company office on Monday, paid up, and had my service restored on Tuesday. Tell Shirley to try me again on her next trip.

Dear Heart, you asked me if the bougainvilleas were still in bloom! Cindy, I love flowers, but if it isn't a rose (or a sunflower), I don't know what it is! I am woefully ignorant, botanically. But flowers of all varieties have been blooming luxuriantly ever since I have been here (six months tomorrow), and I assume they will bloom all year round. I do enjoy them. Incidentally, oddly enough now that I think of it, I don't think I have seen any roses here.

Your interest in Yucatan has (re)stirred my own, and I tentatively plan to make a trip there this winter. Your experiences sound very much like Margaret related of hers. You two would enjoy getting together, reminiscing and showing each other your pictures. I know what you mean about the beautiful blue-green colors of the Caribbean. A few summers ago I spent two weeks on one of the islands of the Antilles, whose name I cannot now remember—a small isle, half of it administered by France, the other half by the Netherlands. St. Something—maybe you know it. Anyway, the prettiest sea waters I have ever seen. The following summer I was two weeks in Bermuda, and though not strictly in the Caribbean (farther north), the water was also beautiful. Of course Bermuda is much more "civilized" than _____,which was much less developed and almost primitive. St. Helen, I think, or maybe I have it confused with that volcano in Oregon. Senility is setting in! I made those trips on the last of the accumulated Pan-Am World pass mileage.

Cindy, I have no more problems talking about my WWII experiences, and my stint as a POW, but it is such ancient history, and I have forgotten many of the details. Of course I remember the constant terror and fear of not living through it, which everybody experienced. Perhaps that could be the subject of my next letter, as this one will grow quite lengthy if I include it here. However, I think it will be helpful to give you some preliminary background here. I don't know how much your dad has told you about the war, or the national ambience existing prior to and during U.S. participation, or how much you have since read about those days, so this may be superfluous.

Your father and I graduated from high school together in June 1941 [in the small town of Fluvanna, Texas. Population at that time was less than 400.] Early in my school years I had skipped a grade, and one year your father dropped out to go around the country with a friend on a motorcycle. When he returned, I talked him into going back to school, and so we were in the same class the last two years of high school.

He turned 18 in May of that year, and almost immediately upon graduation, joined the U.S. Army Air Corps. He went to Kelly Field in San Antonio, and attended aircraft mechanics school. I was only 16 and went to Texas Tech [in Lubbock] that September (I turned 17 in November).

As you know, the Japanese bombed Pearl Harbor on December 7th and the United States was in the war up to its ears. Stories of Hitler's atrocities to the Jews and conquered people were already known in the States (not to the extent revealed after the war), and patriotic fervor was rampant.

I think the U.S. was the most united in anger and purpose during those years than at any other time in its history, or since. Recruiting offices were jammed with long lines of volunteers and the country began putting all its efforts building training camps, air bases and the like, and manufacturing ships, airplanes, tanks and ammunitions. The war was the number one priority for everyone and everyone wanted to do his share.

The Texas Tech campus became almost bare of men except for a few youngsters like me. Your dad was accepted into flying training as a cadet and finally became a second lieutenant pilot. I know he was miserable at never getting sent overseas until after the war when he flew the Berlin Airlift.

Our dad joined the Army Corps of Engineers in June 1942 and was sent to England to help build bases there. [Editor's note: "Dad" is my grandfather, who was 42 years old when he joined the Corps of Engineers. It was common at the time for all the men of a family to go off to war, leaving the women behind.] Our mother and sister moved to Lubbock, Texas, to stay with me, and Mother became a riveter at what is now Reese Air Force Base, working in the sheet metal shop, repairing damaged airplanes. Our sister, Sug [Wanda; her nickname was short for Sugar], was in Lubbock High School and I started my second year at Texas Tech in September 1942 at 17 years old. I was the only "man" in the family left and afraid that the war would be over before I was old enough to enlist.

Mother and I bought that little house on 29th Street, just a block off (then) College Avenue. Do you remember that house at all? College Avenue was only a small two-lane street paved only as far as 24th Street. 34th Street was the absolute south end of town. We managed to buy the tiny place with Mother's salary, money Dad was sending from England, and what money I earned working as a kitchen steward at the downtown Hilton Hotel. I worked full-time and went to college with a full load. I earned $72 per month plus meals from the kitchen. I believe we paid $3,750 for the little house on 29th Street.

Well, to make a long story (a little) shorter, I turned 18 in

November 1942, finished the current semester at Tech in January '43, and went into the service on February 9th, Mother's 38th birthday. Mother and Sug were well settled and no longer needed my contributions to keep up with the mortgage.

At the time I went into the service you could no longer "volunteer" for a particular branch of the service. You were inducted into the "Armed Services," then assigned according to service needs and the results of a long series of "aptitude tests." You could list your preferences, so I listed the Army Infantry, then the Marines, thinking either of those two would be the quickest paths to action.

In their infinite wisdom and based on the results of the aptitude tests, they assigned me to the U.S. Army Air Corps and sent me Scott Field, Illinois, for training as an aircraft radio operator/mechanic. This was after basic training at Sheppard Air Force Base in Wichita Falls [Texas]. I was terribly disappointed not to have been assigned to some fighting unit.

Enough of this gripping saga for now. Do you want me to continue?

Write when you can. I love getting your letters.

Your lovin' Unc

Chapter 4
Other Subjects
"I was going to resume my gripping tale of 'My Life as a Boy Hero' but I have rambled on so long..."

Houston, Texas
November 25, 1988

Dear Weldon,

YES, YES, BY ALL MEANS, PLEASE CONTINUE YOUR STORY. Your last letter ended like a television season-end cliffhanger that they use to get the viewers back in the fall! I am soaking up all the details and observations that you are providing. And learning some things, too. For instance, I didn't know Dad dropped out of school a while to travel the country on a motorcycle with a friend. I like that. I don't really know why. Please continue your story for as long as it may take. Don't leave anything out!

Yes, Shirley missed you when she was there. They were busy getting the villa in order for Thanksgiving visitors. Shirley told me the bougainvillea were not blooming at this time. Weldon, wait till you see the bougainvilleas in January!

If I have any talent for writing, I know now where it must have come from—somewhere in the Squyres line as you evidenced.

That island in the Antilles might be Martinique, or San Martinique. Does that sound familiar?

I will be in Matzatlan January 9-13. I will be staying at the Holiday Inn at Matzatlan with Ted, and his wife, Betty. It is a short trip—we plan to charter a boat for two days and go billfishing. Please join us if at all possible. Ted and Betty are avid fishermen (Betty has participated in women's sailfishing tournaments), but they have never been to Mexico except for one trip to Acapulco some years ago. They are a delightful couple and fun to be around. They hope to be able to meet you and we sure hope you can join us there.

This will be a short letter. Next time you talk to Grandma, please tell her that I got her letter and that I have written to Uncle B. I will write her and Granddad soon. I went to work part-time for the ad agency this past week and with school and the holidays coming up, I'm getting behind in my correspondence. Please continue to write and let me know if we will see you in January in Matzatlan!

Love,
Cindy

Manzanillo, Colima, Mexico
7 de Diciembre 1988 [December 7, 1988]

Mia Querida Sobrina Cindy Lou,

Big doings—big EXCITEMENT in our little town the past couple of weeks. A movie company from Mexico City is in town shooting a movie, or at least some scenes for a movie. They are shooting mostly downtown in and around the old Hotel Colonial, where I stayed for nine days when I first came down here. It must be a "period" picture as they have covered the downtown street with dirt and sand, and brought in a fleet of old 1935-1940 cars, Fords, Hudsons, Packards, etc. Of course everybody in town crowds around as close as they can get to watch the goings-on. They have completely disrupted downtown traffic, both car and pedestrian, and I'll be glad when they're finished, but then, I'm an Old Grouch.

Much more exciting to me—day before yesterday evening a pod of dolphins showed up in the bay, just beyond my front yard seawall, not more than a 100 feet beyond where the waves were breaking. There were 8 to 10 of them, just rolling and splashing, jumping clear out of the water at times, and looking like they were just having fun. They swam up and down the beach for a long time, and I sat on the sea wall with my binoculars, watching them. Four of them were still here the next day (yesterday) and hung around most of the day so I spent most of the day on the seawall. My upstairs neighbor who is a big fisherman and knows these waters well, said they were probably feeding on sardines which seem to inhabit the bay in large numbers. The dolphins must have eaten them all up, or at least had their fill, as I have not seen them today. I am told that occasionally some gray whales will drift into the bay. These are the ones that migrate yearly from Alaska down the Pacific Coast to the Gulf of California, around the tip of Baja. Many of them stay and calve in the Gulf, but evidently some of them come further south. I used to see them from time to time in California, but have yet to see any here.

That island in the Antilles, half Dutch-half French, is St. Martin.

In Dutch, Saint Maarten. Thank you for mentioning Martinique, that made me think of it.

In one of your letters you mention black "parrot-like" birds called anis. There is a large flock of big, black birds that hang around the trees of the apartments, but I wouldn't call them "parrot-like." They are about the size of a large jay, but have longer tails, and bright yellow eyes. They are as bold as brass, and scrappy, like jays. They make a God-awful assortment of noises, squawks, shrieks, whistles, etc., but at times—I guess when they're not feeling so "pecky"—they have a beautiful song. Are these your "anis"?

There is also a very large flock of white herons that stay in a marsh between here and town. At one time, I thought there must be some flamingos in with them, although they were much smaller, and didn't have the hooked beak of the only flamingos I know. Now I notice that they are losing their pink and turning white, so I have concluded that young herons must be pink. Does that square with your bird book? Once I thought I saw a great blue heron in the marsh, but I couldn't be sure, and when I came back by on the bus, I didn't see him. There was one in Santa Barbara I used to see quite often in some marshes not far from the university. Aren't they kind of rare? Another thing puzzles me, all the pelicans and frigate birds have disappeared. They must be migratory, but if I were a seabird, I'm damned if I could think of a place I had rather be!

Dear Heart, thank you for the invitation to join your group in Mazatlan in January. I would dearly love to, but don't think I will be able to make it this time. I'm leaving for California on Saturday, December 17, and will be away for quite awhile. I have some business to tend to in Cal—have to see my tax man and financial advisor, etc., etc. and will stay for Christmas with the kids. (Well parents never stop calling their children "kids"? Lee is 41!) Lee and Judy recently sold their house in Fresno and moved across the Bay to Hayward. We will all be together for Christmas at Drew's and Annamarie's house. Brian and Jeri were transferred the 1st of October from Abilene to Lowry AFB in Denver. They don't think they'll be able to make it home for Xmas, so I will probably stop off in Denver for a few days on my way to Lubbock. Will spend maybe a week with the folks, a day or two in Dallas with friends, then back here. By then you will have caught all the "bills" off the coast of Mazatlan and gone home! You must make your next trip to Mexico to Manzanillo!

By the way, Cindy, I am reading a *most* interesting book about Mexico that you must read if you haven't already. It's called "Distant Neighbors" by Alan Riding who was a *New York Times* reporter in Mexico for 12 years. It's copyrighted in 1984 so is pretty well up-to-date. Incidentally, I will get myself a Mexican bird book while I'm in the States.

You were wondering earlier about coral reef damage due to Hurricane Gilbert. I am enclosing some (now old) clippings that I meant to send you in my last letter. They detail a bit of the damage that Gilbert did to the Yucatan coastline.

I was going to resume my gripping tale of "My Life as a Boy Hero" but I have rambled on so long in this letter that I will wait until the next one and devote it to the continuation. I do hope you all have a wonderful Christmas and a Happy New Year, and lots of *buena suerte* on your fishing trip. Please give my love to *all* your family.

Your lovin' Tio,
Weldon

Chapter 5
The Saga Continues
"But I was still young (and dumb) and eager to see combat..."

Manzanillo, Colima, Mexico
10 de Diciembre, 1988 [December 10, 1988]

Querida Cindy Lou,

I don't remember for sure where I left this tale, so some of this may be repetitious.

On February 9, 1943, one year and two months plus two days after Pearl Harbor, and exactly three months after my 18th birthday, I was sworn into the Armed Services.

I had been very much afraid the military would not take me. You see, I had been born with a congenital tendency toward a certain bone defect. I wasn't born with the defect itself, just the tendency. This tendency was aggravated when we lived in the little town of Barnhart, Texas, and I jumped off the top of a barn at 4 or 5 years old on a dare. My knees came up and struck me very sharply in the chest as I landed flat-footed. Within a year, my chest began to develop a depression in the center. The chest bone (the sternum) to which the right and left ribs attach, is normally flat in the chest. In my case, the left ribs as they came around to attach to the sternum, instead of coming around straight, began to curve further inward, causing the sternum to "cant" inward instead of remaining flat and causing a deepening depression in my chest as I grew older.

Mother and Dad took me to many doctors over the years. Very little was known of genetics then and no one was able to diagnose the cause of the depression growing in my chest. I think there must have been some incompatible genes between Mother and Dad which I surmise might be why Sug was born with a hare lip and cleft palate and why Mother gave birth to a stillborn baby. I don't know if your father ever told you about that. Anyway, your father was the only child who escaped physical problems of the three of us who lived.

My problem never bothered me physically, although I suffered psychological scars growing up, playing sports, showering in the locker room, swimming, etc., and having to answer questions about the depression in my chest. But I led a full, normal, physical, active hardworking life (ask your dad about our boyhood work activities), working from the standard "can see to cain't see" day on farm and ranch. But as my first sophomore semester came to an end at Texas Tech, and as I went to the recruiting office to enlist in either the Infantry or the Marines, my heart was in my mouth fearing that they would not take me at all, simply because of the *appearance* of my sunken chest. I was very fearful that they would classify me 4-F.

Well, they didn't, and in their infinite wisdom instead of assigning me to the Infantry or the Marines, they assigned me to the Army Air Force and sent me for basic training to Shepherd AFB in Wichita Falls, Texas. I have always held that, if you wanted to give the world an enema, Wichita Falls, Texas, would be where you inserted the probe. Having lived and visited there subsequently, nothing has happened to change my mind.

Basic training at Shepherd was largely Infantry type B.T. (The Air Force was still part of the Army at that time). Marching, close order drills, heavy calisthenics, obstacle courses with full pack, bivouacs, living in the field, rifle and pistol range firing. I qualified "expert" (highest rating) with the rifle due to my experiences hunting rabbit as a youngster, but only as a "marksman" (lowest rating) with the .45 caliber automatic pistol simply because that mother was so big and heavy and has so much recoil, you couldn't kill anyone with it except at very close range.

After testing at Fort Sill, Oklahoma (Indoctrination Center) and further testing at Shepherd during Basics, I had been assigned to

Scott Field, Illinois, for training as an aircraft radio operator/ mechanic and completion of basic. So, up to Scott Field via troop train from Shepherd at completion of basic training.

After basic training, life at Scott Field seemed absolutely marvelous. A daily hour of calisthenics was the only required physical activity apart from an occasional formal dress parade for some visiting military VIP. For me, the classes were thoroughly enjoyable.

The "operating" part of the course consisted of learning (sending and receiving) Morse Code, and learning service operational procedures. In code, I got up to 35 words per minute, which is about as fast as a person can take code with a pencil, and was the top speed transmitted though the school. Faster than that you had to go to an advance school in Madison, Wisconsin, and learn to take code on a "mill" (a typewriter). The "mechanics" part of the course was basic electronics theory with emphasis on communications electronics. We also learned specifics of various types of radios in use by the Air Force and the applications of each.

St. Louis was our weekend pass city, just across and up the river from Scott and it was a great town, everything half-priced to guys in uniform. At Old Sportsman Park where the St. Louis Browns and Cardinals both played, you could get in the bleacher seats for free. Great USO dances and shows were held. The local "Clooney Family" starring a very young girl named Rosemary played, and The King Cole Trio from East St. Louis came as well.

After graduating from Scott, there were three options for further training: 1) high-speed code and operations school where cryptography and advanced electronics were offered and became part of the vast radio communications network that was growing around the world; 2) air controllers school, which then offered advanced electronics; or 3) aerial gunnery school for a position on a bomber crew as Radio Operator/Gunner. Both the first two had great appeal to me as I had become very interested in radio at Scott and had graduated fully qualified for either school. But I was still young (and dumb) and eager to see combat, so I applied for option 3 and discovered why I had been assigned to the Air Corps instead of the Infantry or Marines.

I had been put on a classification of "limited services" because of my chest condition and there were more so-called "limited service" jobs available in the Air Corps. Limited service meant some kind of clerk or desk job—no combat. Well, I was crushed and also highly pissed off. Theoretically, I could have been excused from all physical activities during basic training—no marching, no hikes, no physical exercise, etc. I could have just sat in the day room and read, or in the PX and drunk beer. I could have skipped all the parades and basic training to boot.

Well, to try to make a long story a little shorter, I started through the chain of medical command at Scott trying to convince them of the unfairness and illogic that had been done to me, and finally convinced them to let me take the requisite physical exam for gunnery school, which I passed with flying colors. I really had wanted to apply for flying cadet school, but by this time in the war, they had such a long waiting list of applicants, they weren't taking any more. So, I was just as happy to go to the aerial gunnery school at Kingman Air Force Base in Arizona.

Dear Heart, if this is "more than you really wanted to know" about my military career, skip whatever you like—but you said in your last letter "don't leave anything out"—so I will try to remember everything.

The curriculum at gunnery school was so varied it is difficult to describe. First, there was the classwork, from ballistic principles to aircraft recognition. In ballistics, we learned all about muzzle velocities, ballistic paths of projectiles, theories firing at a moving target from a moving base, etc. In "aircraft rec" we learned to identify all the known aircraft in the world, both friendly and hostile. This was done through a series of slide presentations, in ever decreasing exposure times, of aircraft from every possible angle of perception. For instance, slides had differing numbers of aircraft, viewed from different angles. We had to identify each aircraft in every slide, indicate the number of each type of aircraft in slides with a large number of aircraft of many different types and from different perspectives in exposure times of fractions of seconds. It all required intense and prolonged concentration.

In the field, we learned to field strip, then detail strip and reassemble .50 caliber machine guns and to learn and be able to recite the mechanical function of each piece. To field strip (and re-assemble) is to take down its major subassemblies. To detail strip a gun is to take it down to its everlasting single piece, and then explain the function of each piece, to reassemble and fire it. Finally, we had to do this *blindfolded* in a timed test! I loved it! It was not really as hard as it sounds since a .50 caliber machine gun is a relatively simple mechanism.

One of the best parts of gunnery school was skeet shooting. Part of the course was regular, standard skeet with .12 gauge shotguns and regulation "low" house and "high" house skeet releases. This was to teach shooting at a moving target (although from a stationary base), and although I had never shot skeet before, I had hunted rabbits with a .12 gauge shotgun as well as with a 22 rifle, and I did quite well.

The next step was shooting at a moving target from a *moving base*. This was accomplished through the means of a 10- or 12-mile irregular oval track road with skeet houses at irregular spacings and untimed release times. Shooters were in the back of a G.I. pickup truck with assigned firing rotations. The truck was traveling at 10 or 15 mph, and you had to get your birds without warning as to timing of release or direction of flight. I *loved* it, thought it great sport and did well.

On the machine gun firing line, we fired (from a stationary base) at moving targets at various distances pulled by little trolley cars going at varying speeds. Scores were kept by wet paint-tipped bullets of various colors. In the air (moving target from moving base), we fired from various turret and hand-held positions, at a tow target pulled by a B-26 bomber, at various distances and speeds relative to ours. For a while, your dad flew such a B-26 bomber in Tampa, Florida at a gunnery school.

On the ground, further gunnery training included sessions in turret and hand-held shooting in "penny arcade" galleries, where we fired at make-believe incoming hostiles, with our scores electronically recorded. In addition to all this, our physical training was intense, with heavy emphasis on calisthenics, obstacle courses, etc. I finished gunnery training at age 18 in the best physical shape that I had ever been in before or since!

Next, graduation from gunnery school (with the rank of Sgt.), assignment to Westover Air Force Base (near Springfield, Mass.), and a 10-day delay in route to Westover. Took a civilian train from Kingman, Arizona, to Amarillo [Texas]. Bus to Lubbock for my first leave since joining up. I caught up on the details of Dad's and Lec's (your dad) adventures (mail had been sporadic) and enjoyed visiting with the very few old friends who were left in Lubbock.

This is growing far too long and detailed, so will try to shorten it up a bit. At Westover, we were assigned to crews for crew training at other bases. A heavy bomber (4 engine) crew consisted of pilot, co-pilot, navigator and bombardier, all of whom were commissioned officers. The navigator and bombardier were most often "washed out" flying cadets, who had elected their respective alternate optional schools in order to gain their commissions. The EM's (enlisted men, all sergeants) were the flight engineer, the radio operator, the armorer, the ball turret gunman, and the tail gunner, who had no other specialties except as gunners. All the crew except the pilot and co-pilot had been to gunnery school.

Early in the war, the navigator and bombardier manned two handheld .50 calibers in the nose. Later airplanes (both B-17's and B-24's) had a nose turret with twin .50s manned by a specialist gunner, and the navigator and bombardier were relieved of gunnery duties. All the turrets (nose, upper, ball and tail) had twin .50's. In the later planes, the only hand-helds were in the waist, one manned by the armorer, the other by the radio operator. The flight engineer manned the upper turret as it was just aft of the flight deck.

My group (from Scott and Kingman) were all assigned to B-24 crews. You seem to know old warplanes so I will not go into much detail about the old "Liberator." The B-17, the "Flying Fortress," got all the publicity during and after the war, but the "Lib" was much faster, carried a heavier bomb load and had a longer range than the Fort. It was not as rugged physically—it could not sustain the damage a Fort could and still fly. If you had to ditch it the ocean, the Lib had a bad (deserved) reputation for the fuselage to break in two right behind the high "Davis" wing and sink very quickly. If it landed properly under favorable conditions, the Fort could stay afloat for awhile, sometimes even long enough for the crew to get out.

After "crewing up" at Westover, we were sent to Chatham Field, Georgia, near Savannah for crew training, then later to Langley Field, Virginia. Crew training consisted of various practice missions, practice bombing runs, navigational training (including radio navigation), formation flying and aerial gunnery practice with a B-25 or B-26 towing a "sock" [target].

We were training as replacement crews as the "Air Forces" (8th in England and 15th in Italy) wings, groups and squadrons were already long since in place. Although the 8th Air Force in England consisted mostly of B-17 groups, later in the war many B-24's were in the 8th. The 15th Air Force based in Southern Italy consisted almost completely of B-24's because of their longer range [capable of making round trips of 1,500 to nearly 2,000 miles].

So, as we completed crew training we were dispatched separately to our overseas assignments. My crew departed from Langley Field, Virginia, in a brand new, latest model B-24 with nose and tail turrets for an overnight stay at Grenier AFB in New Hampshire. (Your family was stationed there for awhile), thence to Gander Bay in Newfoundland, on to a stopover in the Azores, to Marrakech in Morocco, Algiers, Tunis (I may have the order reversed. I don't have a map of North Africa) and finally to Foggia in southern Italy near the Bari on the Adriatic Coast.

The trip over was both exciting and boring. Exciting as we were "on our way" at last—boring with the long hours of flight over seemingly endless expanses of ocean. I read James Hilton's *Lost Horizons* on the way over. I would ride for awhile in the tail turret or the ball turret. Eerie feeling. In the tail turret, the gunner is almost completely out of visual contact with the rest of the ship. About all he can see is the twin vertical stabilizers to each side. In the ball turret, the gunner is even more isolated. In the B-24, the ball turret is retractable. The gunner gets in, then lowers the turret, and in most positions within the turret, he is *completely* isolated from visual contact with the ship. It's very claustrophobic as there is *only* room for your scrunched up bod. Ball turret gunners were always small. Ours was "Shorty" Rogers from Bessmer, Alabama. I never envied ball or tail turret gunners their jobs.

Well, we finally arrived at the base near Foggia and were assigned to the 782nd Squadron, 465th Heavy Bomber Group, 15th Air Force. Our beautiful new Lib was immediately taken over by Squadron Headquarters and assigned to another, older crew.

We were still in for some more "orientation training."

More later.

Abrazos y besos,
Your Unk

Chapter 6
Mexico: Whales and other Tales
"They were quite playful, sometimes leaping completely clear of the water..."

Manzanillo, Colima, Mexico
Domingo, 12 de February 1989 [February 12, 1989]

Querida Sobrina Cindy Lou,

I'm sorry I was not able to join you and friends for fishing in Mazatlan. I did not get back from California and Texas until 14 January. Please write and tell me all about it.

First, let me catch up on some back subjects, birds. I got a Mexican bird book—Roger Tory Peterson's—and am a little disappointed in it as it is somewhat sketchy, referring many varieties to his American books—East, Texas, and West. However, I have his book "Birds of the West," so with both of them, I make out OK.

The big black birds I wrote you about (asking if they might be anis) are boat-tailed grackles. The males are an iridescent black, almost purple in the right sunlight, with long V or keel-shaped tails. The females are smaller, and not nearly so black, almost dark brown.

The pink birds I saw in among the herons are roseate spoonbills. Haven't seen them in a while. I made a new sighting several days ago, which I have tentatively identified as a wood stork or a wood ibis, a large white bird with black on the outer undersides of his wings. Until I can see the black pattern more clearly I can't be real sure. It might be a rare whooping crane that somehow wandered this far south. He appears to be alone. I have not spotted a mate.

Other sea birds I have identified are cormorants, kingfishers, and brown boobies. Of course there are the brown pelicans, and the frigate birds, which I knew from Brazil. I didn't even try to identify the many species of gulls, I think they are *all* here.

Did I tell you about the dolphins? Forgive me if I am repeating myself. Before I left for California, a school of dolphins, eight or ten, appeared in the bay, staying for several days, swimming and cavorting up and down the beach real close in, just beyond where the surge breaks. They were really exciting to watch, and put on quite a show, "porpoising" and sometimes leaping clear of the water! I have since spotted two or three from time to time, but have not seen the large school again.

To add to the aquatic excitement, a few days after I returned from Texas, a "pod" of five or six gray whales appeared in the bay! They didn't come as close in as the dolphins, but quite close enough to see them well. I used to watch them in California during the fall migration, but they were so far offshore about all you could see was a spout and an occasional roll, even with binoculars. These must have wandered down south from Baja and were checking out Manzanillo Bahia. They were quite playful, sometimes leaping completely clear of the water and falling on their backs with a tremendous splash. Or they would surface and give a huge slap of their tail, raising a real rooster tail of water.

I have heard that they do this to get rid of barnacles, but it looks like they are just having fun. The de-barnacling theory makes sense. You know water is nonelastistic and noncompressable; it can only be displaced and with the mass and force with which they hit the water. It's probably pretty hard on the poor damn barnacle. If I were one and saw that mass of whale coming down on me, I would scuttle like hell for the bottom!

These guys stayed around for a few days, then left, I guess to go back to el Golfo de California. I have not seen any since.

Last Thursday (the 9th) was a big day for me. I went deep-sea fishing for the first time! I had been salmon fishing before in Canada, with friends from Vancouver, in the straits between Vancouver Island and the mainland, but as you probably know, it's a completely different kind of fishing. My upstairs "snowbirder" neighbor from Louisville, Kentucky, Tom P——, is an avid sports fisherman, tournament awards, etc., and a couple of friends of his, Bob and Mary G—- from near Kansas City, Missouri, were down for a couple of weeks (also experienced sports fishers) and we went out together. We left the pier at Las Brisas (on the Inner Harbor side) at about 7:00 a.m.

Mary landed the first big "sail" and Tom gave me the next. I had "buck fever" so bad for the first few minutes I didn't know what to do. Bob had one on at the same time, but in the flurry of getting the other lines in and the skipper playing the boat to try to help both of us, Bob's managed to throw the hook. Mine took out about 250 yards of line, surfaced several times and skittered across the water on his tail, tossing his head trying to free the hook. I was yelling like a rodeo cowboy, but with Tom's coaching soon got into the rhythm of pumping and reeling, pumping and reeling. After about 30 minutes of the hardest damn work I have done since picking cotton, we hauled him in.

Tom estimated him at around 60 lbs., and he looked to be almost 6 feet from tip of bill to tail. He had put up such a good fight, I asked them to let him go, which they did. Later when we landed, Tom took a picture of me with Mary's fish, which was about the same size, but which had not put up nearly so much of a fight. (Tom explained that it was the way he had been hooked.) I'll send you a copy when he gets them back.

We got back to the dock about 1:30 and I was totally pooped. It had been tremendous fun and was totally exciting, but I must confess I had rather catch a two-pound trout on a fly line with a 4 or 6 oz. leader, then clean him and pop him in a frying pan!

Yesterday (Sabado) to vary my routine a bit, I took a day trip to Tecoman, about an hour bus ride south, then a local bus about 12 km (approx. 7.5 mi.) down to the Playa Boca de Pascuales. It's known locally for its "ramadas"—thatched roofed, open, seafood restaurants, which stretch for about a third of a mile along a beautiful, noncrowded beach. I was amazed at how few people there were. A waitress told me that on Saturday everyone goes into Tecomon for the market. As the only gringo in the place, I was the object of much curiosity, and lots of labored conversations. I am getting better (Spanish) and such trips where *nobody* speaks English give me a lot of practice. I had a big lunch of shrimp *diablo* garnished with sliced onion, tomatoes and avocados. The *diablo* [devil] sauce was so hot it took three Dos Equis [a Mexican brand name beer] to quench the fire. The whole meal including the three beers was 1300 pesos, now about $5.60. Since the beers were 4500 pesos, the meal itself was about $3.65 and it was almost more shrimp than I could eat, as much as I love shrimp.

I continue to be amazed at how cheap and efficient public transportation is here. The bus fare from here to Tecomon was 1800 pesos—about 78 cents. Local fare from Tecomon to the *playa* [beach] was 500 pesos—22 cents. Buses run between Manzanillo and Tecomon and return every 15 minutes throughout the day! This is why it just doesn't make any kind of economic sense for me to buy a car.

Well Dear Heart—that's about all the news from Mexico. Please write soon about your holidays and the fishing trip to Mazatlan. I look forward to you making a trip down here. Let me know!

Where did I leave off with the wartime saga? I think we had arrived in southern Italy. I will resume that tale soon.

Your loving tio,
Weldon

Chapter 7
June 1944: The Replacement Crew
"It's hard now to believe that I was that green, naïve, romantic, idealistic, and foolish 19-year-old kid..."

Manzanillo, Colima, Mexico
15 de Feb 1989

Dear Heart,

It is getting more difficult to continue with my story—no, don't misunderstand, not because of still painful memories, but from lack of remembrance, especially of the details. Memory is a random phenomenon. It all seems so long ago and far away, that it could have happened in another life, or to someone else and I only heard about it. It is hard now to believe that I was that green, naive, idealistic, and foolish 19-year-old kid who landed in southern Italy in June 1944. Ike's troops had just landed in Normandy, and Naples had just fallen to the Allied Forces as they fought their way foot-by-foot northward up that bitterly contested peninsula. And here I'd come to save the day. Jesus.

We arrived as a replacement crew and, to a certain extent, as replacement crew members for older crews decimated by losses by death and injury or completion of tour duty. A tour of duty was 50 missions, and on completion of a tour, a crewman was rotated back to the States, usually as an instructor in his military specialty.

Not too many people completed 50 missions, however.

Our pilot, with whom we had trained and flown over, 2nd Lt. Bill Rye from Dallas, was assigned to another crew as co-pilot, much to his (and our) chagrin. We drew a long, tall, lanky Texan from Houston as pilot, 1st Lt. Theodore ("Ted") Poole. Ted was already a veteran of several missions and had lost his crew. I don't remember how.

Our co-pilot, Chuck (I've forgotten his last name), was a young, small, wiry guy from Omaha. He had washed out of fighter school and had been relegated to bombers and carried a huge chip on his shoulder. Our new co-pilot was 1st Lt. Bert Lowenthal, already a veteran of several missions with another crew. Thus, we had two veterans in the cockpit. Our navigator was an older guy named Max Sunshine, appropriately enough from Florida. He was already a captain and had gone through cadet school as an officer. He washed out of cadet training and went to navigation school. All navigators and bombardiers were washouts from flying school. They also went through the same aerial gunnery training as the enlisted crewmen.

Our bombardier was a young 2nd looey from Rozne, New York, named Benjamin ("Benny") P. Benson. The flight engineer was another Texan from Slaton named Nathan ("Tex") Evetts. He was also the top turret gunner. Our armorer and waist gunner was a big, jaw-boned country boy from somewhere near Bismark, North Dakota. His ears had been frost-bitten as a kid, and he had lost the outer edges of both earlobes. His name was Bob Salmon and he was to become one of my best friends on the crew.

The armorer is responsible (along with the bombardier) for overseeing the loading of the bombs prior to a mission. He also has the tricky task during the flight before we reached the I.P. (initial point or beginning of the bomb run) of going into the bomb bay on a narrow catwalk, and "arming" all the bombs. The other two crew members were gunners only with no other military specialties. They were Oscar "Shorty" Rogers from Bessemer, "Alafuckinbama," the ball turret gunner, and Albert ("Al") Hill from Newark, the tail turret gunner.

The first couple of weeks after our arrival and reassignment of Bill Rye to another crew, and assignment of Ted Poole to our crew, was taken up with more orientation and training. I was anxious to get started and felt all of this *fal de ral* was so much shit. Every evening at the Operations Tent, the crews scheduled for the next day's mission were posted on the bulletin board. We all checked it faithfully every evening to see if we had been posted. No luck.

At every posting, there are some crews listed with vacancies among various crew members due to death or injury or completion of tour. Eager beaver volunteers who were trying to complete their tours could volunteer. One evening, Capt. Henderson's crew was lacking a radio operator/gunner. I blithely went into the operations tent and volunteered to fly, never mentioning I had never flown a combat mission (and never being asked!). I was posted for an early wake-up by a runner from Operations, early breakfast and briefing.

Next morning's briefing revealed that the target was Toulon, France, on the southern Mediterranean coast. It was known to be a German submarine tender station where subs guarded the southern Atlantic and Mediterranean against Allied shipping. It was heavily fortified and an important German naval base.

I am going to break off here, as it is 5:00 p.m. and I want to get into town and check the mail and get this into the mail before 6.

Much love,
Skip

Chapter 8
The First Bailout
"I returned to base a much chastened 'war hero'—newly aware that war was not a movie..."

Manzanillo, Colima, Mexico
16 de Feb. 1989

Dear Cindy Lou,

I want to continue this while my brain is still somewhat in gear and my memory is still freshening.

I was awakened that morning by a runner from Operations around 4:00 a.m. After breakfast and briefing, we headed in trucks out to the parking ramps. The briefing had been terse and laconic. I had not known what to expect. We were given flight weather conditions (good), conditions over the target area (weather good, clear, target heavily fortified, no fighter resistance expected), the strategic importance of the target, etc., radio codes, various emergency procedures, and wished "Godspeed." The group chaplin closed with a prayer and we headed out toward the waiting loaded bombers. As I said, I had not known what to expect and it all seemed rather hum-drum and matter-of-fact to me. I guess I had expected more melodramatics—something on the order of *12 O' Clock High* or some of the other wartime air movies.

I was, at the same time, a little disappointed, yet still thrilled with the terse reality of it all. I had made myself known to all my new crew members before and after the briefing, without mentioning that this was my first mission. They accepted me at face value and we made inane pleasantries about where we were all from, where we went to radio school, gunnery school, etc., on the ride out to the waiting ships.

I did not want to know and did not ask what had happened to their previous radio operator/gunner and they did not volunteer the information.

So we arrived at the pad of "Massa's Dragon" and Capt. Henderson gathered us together, made a short welcome to me, recapped the briefing instructions, and we got aboard. We took off, circling to wait for later takeoffs, finally getting into group formation and headed northwest across the Mediterranean Sea toward Toulon, France.

We were accompanied most of the way across by squadrons of P-38 Lightning fighters flown by an all-black group based a little further north of us. I, then and there, lost all my feelings of southern bigotry, and those guardian angels accompanied us on many other trips saving our asses on many occasions from the German ME 109s and FW 190s [fast fighter planes]. Their group commander was Col. Benjamin Hooks, who later became an Air Force General and for many years had been the leader of the NAACP [National Association for the Advancement of Colored People].

We finally arrived at the target and started peeling off to form up on the I.P. [initial point] for the bomb run. We had had no fighter interceptions and the mission had begun to look like a cake walk. Except that ack-ack fire was *very* heavy over the target area. You must remember that this is my first mission, and my "baptism by fire."

At the I.P. the bombardier takes control of the airplane and literally flies it down the bomb run through controls connected to the Norden bomb sight. We can take no evasive action during the bomb run and this is the most dangerous part of a mission except straggling homeward alone with a wounded airplane watching out for enemy fighters.

During the bomb run, the navigator who occupies the nose with the bombardier watches over both the hand-held .50's in the nose and exercises his sphincter muscle a lot as he watches the flak bursts coming closer and closer. The bomb run was known as "flak alley." [Flak was pieces of metal shot into the sky to down airplanes. This originated the expression "catching flak" or criticism.] The Brits had invented radar, but the Germans were not far behind with it and their ack-ack guns at the major targets were radio controlled. You could see the tracking pattern as the flak bursts came closer and closer during the bomb run, as we had to fly a straight course. The nose must have been the scariest place in the whole damned airplane—not for the bombardier—he was busy as hell, but for the navigator, who watches the flak coming closer and there is nothing between him and that lethal steel but a thin sheet of plastic canopy.

You could hear the bursts explode—they give off a dull sounding "whoomph whoomph"—then you hear the shrapnel hit against metal and plastic—it sounds like hail on a tin roof. You can see them tracking you.

I am thinking, *My God, those bastards are trying to kill me!* and all I am doing is sitting up here trying to knock out their submarine pens. You watch the bursts come closer and you hear the "whoomph! whoomph!" and you hear the hail on the tin roof and you shrivel up inside yourself in terror. A flak burst explodes under a wing and you almost do a complete roll over. An engine catches fire and is feathered by the pilot. Another flak burst catches you under the other wing and again you almost roll over. Finally, the bombardier hollers "bombs away!" The pilot takes over and we peel off on two engines, unable to form up with the rest of the group for flight home.

We straggle home, keeping a sharp lookout for fighters which we do not see, thank God.

The navigator sets a course back across the Mediterranean Sea that hopefully will take us south of Naples. We are flying a descending course on two engines, hoping we will not have to ditch. The B-24 has a very poor record of ditching at sea. The fuselage has a way of breaking in two right behind the high Davis wing, and sinking rapidly. The B-17 Fort has a very good record of staying afloat for a long time, giving plenty of time for escape. So, we watch, and wait.

Finally, we see the coast of Italy and Capt. Henderson instructs all to bail out as soon as we hit the coast. The tail gunner, the ball turret gunner and the waist gunner all bailed out too quickly and landed in the drink, but were later picked up by Italian fishermen. I was too damned scared to go out too soon, and was the last person out aft. I reported to Capt. Henderson that everybody aft was out, and I was going.

I went out through the waist hatch and waited the required three seconds to clear the ship and pulled my ripcord. There is just exactly time enough to think between the time you pull the ripcord and the chute opens to think, *Oh my God, it isn't going to open.* Then it opens and you remember with startling clarity why they say to wear your chute harness very tightly cinched!

I landed in a vineyard surrounded by Italian *paisanos* and when I identified myself as an Americano, I was hailed as a conquering hero! The rest of the crew was picked up by a group of U.S. Engineer Corpsmen who were "sapping" the Anzio beachhead of mines (anti-personnel). They took us up to Naples where the next day a ship from our group came to pick us up. I returned to base a much chastened "war hero"—newly aware that war was not a movie, and that life was precious.

More later,
Skip

Manzanillo, Colima, Mexico
17 de Feb. 1989

Querida Sobrina Cindy Lou,

We arrived back at camp near Foggia from Naples late the following day. When we didn't return with the group, everyone thought we had "bought the farm" as several planes and crews had been lost over the target. Then finally Capt. Henderson had been able to get through by radiophone from Naples late that evening and my crew members, who had been sweating me out, were particularly relieved. The squadron sent a plane up to Naples to pick us up. On the ride back I had told Capt. Henderson and the rest of his crew that that had been my first mission, and they were astounded that I should have been so stupid as to volunteer for a mission to Toulon. Volunteers were usually only available for what we called "milk runs." But I had not known that Toulon was such an important and well defended target until it was too late.

The reaction of my own crew was mixed. At the same time, they were a little in awe of what I had done and what had happened to me, but also a little scornful that I had done such a damnfool thing as volunteer for something—a very un-Army concept!

Capt. Henderson commended me for my actions in the waist prior to bail out to Ted Poole, and to the Group Commander, whose name I don't remember.

After chow that night, we stopped by the Ops Tent to check the bulletin board and, sure enough, our crew was scheduled to go out the very next day! There was a "volunteer needed" for R.O.G. (radio operator/gunner) as I hadn't been expected back. I went in to the Ops Officer and "volunteered" for my own spot. He laughed and told me I could beg off if I wanted to (he had heard of my escapade. Indeed, the whole damn camp had!) but I told him no, I wanted to fly with my crew on its first mission.

The next day was a milk run to somewhere up in northern Italy. I don't even remember the target, but we encountered no fighters (we had our P-38 escorts) and the flak over the target was light compared to Toulon. We were not touched, but Hon, the *fear* was *always* there! Milk runs can turn into tragedies. Fighters can come out of the sun— out of nowhere. There is always a flak burst that can hit the vital innards of your fragile airplane—a large assemblage of metal, plastic, and fearful human beings.

Fear is a funny thing. It was *never* talked about, but it was always there and everybody felt it—everybody had it. If you didn't, you had to be a Section 8 (crazy!) I guess bravery and heroism—hard qualities to define—are persistent in going ahead with the job to be done, to do what you have to do, and were trained well to do, to keep flying mission after mission, milk run or hell, in spite of the ever-clutching fear and terror of mutilation, death and destruction. That first mission I flew changed for good my childish romanticism, and dreams of heroic glory, and in one day I grew several years in wisdom and knowledge of reality.

I don't remember any other milk runs. I think those were reserved for new crews' first missions. We flew to southern France (Toulon again), southern Germany, northern Italy, to Yugoslavia and Romania. The oil fields and refineries clustered around Ploesti in German-occupied Romania were the most heavily fortified targets in all Europe. These were the primary sources of Germany's fuel supply on which she depended to wage her total war. The saying was that the flak was so thick over Ploesti, the birds could walk!

Unfortunately, airplanes couldn't. We went there twice. Pure hell, both times, but we got back when many didn't.

We watched other ships taking direct hits and falling apart in the air—wings, engines, tail sections falling, windmilling in the air, and you try to identify them, and count the number of chutes opening for later debriefing.

Fighters were not so much of a problem. Remember, we were in the last year of the war and the German Luftwaffe had been largely whipped, mainly by the R.A.F. [British Royal Air Force]. We had our black guardian angels, the P-38 Lightenings, who were able to accompany us most of the way to our targets, and who could pick us up at some point on our return. On the way out to target, tight, rigidly-disciplined formation flying offered a great deal of protection. Each B-24 had two hand-held 50s in the nose, two 50s in the upper turret, two hand-held 50s in the waist, two 50s in the ball turret underneath, and two 50s in the tail turret. In tight formation we formed a phalanx few enemy fighters tried to penetrate.

[About the B-24 Liberator: It was a four-engine bomber that carried a crew of ten. Most versions included the ten 50-caliber machine guns, as described above. Its gross weight when loaded and armed was more than 60,000 pounds. It was powered by four 1,200 hp engines and carried 2,750 gallons of fuel, giving it the capability of making round trips of 1,500-2,000 miles. The most common bomb load was ten 500-pound bombs or five 1,000-pound bombs.

During the war in Europe, it usually flew at altitudes of 18,000-28,000 feet. The planes were not pressurized or heated. Crew members had to wear oxygen masks on high-altitude missions, and were exposed to freezing temperatures that could be more than 30 degrees below 0 Fahrenheit.

The B-24 Liberator was produced in greater numbers (a total of 19,256 between 1939 and 1945) and flown in combat by more countries than any other four-engine bomber, including the more famous B-17 "Flying Fortress." The Liberator, which could fly higher, faster, farther, carry more bombs and take more punishment from enemy fire, was affectionately, but unglamorously, called the "Box Car" by those who flew in her. At the beginning of the 21st century, there were reportedly only two flight-worthy B-24s left in the world.]

It was coming home that we were most vulnerable. Shot to hell over the target, planes missing, planes suffering varying degrees of damage and flyability, unable to re-form in the same tight group, we straggled all over the sky and were sitting ducks for the fighters who waited for us, first after the target and before our escorts could rejoin us. This was when, and how we lost most of bombers to fighters, and this is what happened to me later in my story.

In camp when you weren't flying, life was fairly good. You adopted a somewhat fatalistic day-to-day attitude. When you weren't flying, you were not likely to get killed so fear receded (but did not disappear—you could always be flying the next day!).

Chow was pretty good. Usually powdered scrambled eggs for breakfast or what was called S.O.S. which everybody purported to hate, but I frankly liked. It was creamed chipped beef (dried) on toast, which was called "shit on a shingle." (Service people are very graphic.) We had lots of local Italian fruits and vegetables. (Southern Italy was mostly agricultural, fresh chicken, pork, etc.)

The Group had gathered together much abandoned German equipment—motorcycles, gasoline, trucks, etc., and we had Italian speaking G.I.'s who would made regular trips around the countryside picking up fresh eggs, Dago Red and Purple Death (homemade vino), and various other local delights. Every tent (actually a wood-floored structure with wooden half-walls and a canvas top, quite large) had its own homemade cast iron, gasoline fed (Jerry gas) stove for cooking, and we lived quite well. If you were not scheduled to fly, your time was your own and there were many trips into Foggia and over to the Adriatic Coast for sunbathing and body surfing. Except for the war, life was great!

We had a P.X. [Post Exchange—originally the general store of an outpost or fort] ration of four cans of beer a week, but we had no ice. Many different schemes were concocted for cooling beer, but none of them worked in the summer heat of southern Italy. I finally arrived at the fine idea of taking my beer on the next mission. At 20 to 25,000 feet of altitude, unheated, unpressurized, the beer would get plenty damn cold. When we came down to 10,000 feet and came off oxygen, I would enjoy a nice cold beer. I opened a can and in two seconds, the whole can of beer was all over the waist of the ship! Thus do we learn about physics and the expansion of liquids under low pressure!

Flying at high altitudes in an unpressurized, unheated plane had its own problems besides the pervading fear of what you were doing and where you were going. In spite of fur-lined boots and flying suits, you were *cold.* Your feet froze in spite of heavy stamping. Inside your oxygen mask, your nose runs and drips and freezes. You have to continually lift your mask and wipe your nose and mouth with your frozen woolen-gloved hand. It gets sore.

Through the open waist window, the slip stream makes different songs under the ear flaps of your flying helmet. The most persistent was an old gospel hymn: "Be not dismayed what e'er betide, God will take care of you..." This rang in my ears on almost all my missions.

Tio,
Skip

Chapter 9
The Second Bailout
"Oh my God—I'm hit."

Manzanillo, Colima, Mexico
26 de Feb. 1989

Dear Cindy Lou,

I should have continued the saga when I was in the mood. Now, for some reason, it is more difficult. I don't think it is any subconscious reluctance. I am just getting tired of it. Tired of writing, tired of trying to rack my brain for the old memories, many of which elude me. I haven't thought as much and as hard about all these events for many years until I started putting it down on paper for you.

There had been rumors floating around the base for several days of a pending big, important raid—a massive effort. Everyone assumed it was another trip to Ploesti, and there were a lot of tight, drawn faces in camp. Then, on the evening of August 2, 1944, we saw at the Ops Tent that the whole 782nd Squadron was posted for tomorrow's mission.

The next morning at briefing, we learned the entire 465th Heavy Bomb Group was posted and several other groups from the 15th Air Force. The target was Frederickshaefen, Germany, near Lake Constance on the Swiss border. It was to be a long mission as it was just about at the limit of a loaded Liberator range.

The military target was aircraft factories. Both Messerschmidt and Focke-Wulff had factories there where they built the ME 109s and the FW 190s. The strategic purpose was to further reduce the

Luftwaffe's already weakened power and to deter their capability for fighter support of the fierce ground battles that continued after the D-Day Invasion [June 6, 1944], both in France and northern Italy.

We were briefed to expect fighter interception and that the targets were heavily fortified with anti-aircraft guns. Our P-38 escorts could not accompany us much more than halfway. We were told to regroup as fast as possible after the bomb run and to keep tight formations on the way home. (Of course that was standard procedure on any mission, but difficult to do at heavily defended targets!)

So, early on the morning of August 3rd we took off, circled and waited until the whole group could form up and finally took off north for Germany, everybody with tight sphincter muscles. This was my 19th mission. But there was reassurance in looking out the waist window on both sides at that vast armada of airplanes, on each side, aft and ahead. We looked almost invulnerable and the targets were due to take a heavy pounding.

We finally neared the targets and started peeling off at the I.P. for the bomb runs. The flak was terrible, almost equal to Ploesti. Ship after ship was hit to greater or lesser degrees, some exploding with wings, tails, engines and fuselages cartwheeling through the air. Some suffered lesser damage, dropped their bombs and staggered off in the general direction of home [Italy], many crews bailing out after they had left the target. We were heavily buffeted but took no vital hits. There was some safety in numbers—the Germans only had so many guns and we were in a contingent of a huge part of the whole 15th Air Force. So we completed our run, turned tail and started forming up with other survivors. On the way home, we could not fly a tight formation, as many ships had differing degrees of flyability, so we loitered with the stragglers and tried to keep the best formation we could.

In the Udine River valley of northern Italy, Goering had stationed crack squadrons of ME 109s and FW 190s, all with their noses painted a bright yellow—the "yellow noses." These squadrons were lying in wait for us on the way back, hidden in the sun high above us. They struck our struggling echelon with a suddenness and ferocity that I cannot begin to describe.

The air was filled with the scream of fighter engines and bursts of machine gun and 20mm cannon fire. As the yellow noses zoomed down from overhead, Shorty Rogers got off a couple of busts from the ball turret as they zoomed past below us. Almost immediately, Bert Lowenthal was on the intercom. He had lost control of the Liberator.

We were among the first hit and within seconds our B-24 was ablaze in a mass of flames. The German fighters use a percentage of tracer bullets among the regular ammo and when one of those hits the oxygen tanks stored over the bomb bay, the ship is doomed as of course pure oxygen is a great feeder of fire and the extreme heat will melt aluminum.

"Bail out! Now!" screamed Bert Lowenthal over the intercom. Ted Poole was killed instantly. My adrenaline is pumping hard. I am strangely unmoved by Ted's death. Bob Salmon is helping Shorty Rogers up out of the ball turret. I go to the tail turret to help Al Hill. He is dead with blood all over the turret. As the plane begins to pitch wildly, I struggle back to the waist to help Bob and Shorty. Shorty jumps out and Bob grabs for his chute. (We wore harnesses but not chutes. The chute is a "chest" chute that quickly clamps onto your harness.) In the flames and smoke engulfing the plane, Bob grabs his chute by the rip cord and spills it out into the waist and it catches fire.

We both grab it up and beat out the flames and Bob gathers it up in his arms and goes out the waist window. I watch him fall and realize I am still on intercom. I report that Al and Ted are dead, everyone else aft is out, and I am going. There is no reply from the cockpit.

I am alone.

I go out the waist window, still hooked to the intercom line and the oxygen system. I forgot to unhook! As I go out the waist, worrying about hitting the tail vertical stabilizer, the elastic straps on my oxygen mask stretch to their limits until the hose connection lets go and the mask flies back to my face, bloodying my nose and stunning me momentarily. I come to quickly, feeling, smelling and tasting the blood and thinking for a moment, *Oh my God, I'm hit.*

Then I realize what happened and almost laugh. The sounds of the air battle are still all around me and I delay opening my chute. German fighter pilots have been known to shoot Allied fliers in their chutes. My own calm surprises me. I calculate about how far I could safely fall before opening my chute. Catching occasional glimpses of the ground through the clouds, I delay as long as possible and finally pull the rip cord. After the now familiar "oh shit" interval, the chute opens and I oscillate in the wind down to the ground somewhere in the southern Alps. My oscillation was luckily timed so that I had a fairly gentle landing against a fairly steep slope. I doff my chute and bury it under leaves, clean up the blood from my nose and face as best I can and start my way up slope. I had seen another parachute land up there and thought it might be Bob Salmon.

After almost an hour to reconnoiter 200 yards, I finally reached the spot and my heart sank. The figure was lying very still, his parachute partly caught in the trees with a lot of blood around. It was not Bob, but another guy from my squadron whose name I can't remember. He had taken a machine gun bullet through the fleshy part of his thigh, was unconscious, and still bleeding badly. His leg was almost blown off.

I undid him from his chute, got out the first aid kit and gave him a shot of morphine and put a tourniquet on his leg, then disentangled his chute and was in the process of burying it when a heavily German accented voice behind me said, "Put up hands!"

I put up my hands, turned around slowly and faced six or seven German civilian mountaineers all carrying rifles aimed at me. The spokesman said, "Now for you the war is over." He nor I realized it, but it had only entered a new phase. I told them my comrade was badly wounded and needed medical attention. The leader dispatched one of the others who soon returned with a litter of sorts and we started down the mountain taking turns bearing the wounded and dying G.I.

Finally, we reached the little village of Ehrwald. I was put into a cell in the little village jail, soon to be joined by a number of others.

I never knew or was able to find out what happened to my squadron mate. I would guess he finally died from loss of blood and shock.

The people of those mountains had heard and witnessed the air battle above them and had spotted the chutes coming down and had sent out groups to search and intercept them. Before the day was ended, there were eleven of us in the Ehrwald jail, including my co-pilot Bert Lowenthal. The rest were from my squadron or the Bomb Group.

It was then, as we recounted what had just happened, did the gravity of reality became so pervasive. We all had some form of the shakes. Speculation about and contemplation of our uncertain future caused the icy fingers of dread to grip our hearts. Bert and I wondered what had happened to Max and Benny. Bert had seen them jump. We wondered too about Bob Salmon after I told Bert about the chute fire. We talked about Ted Poole and Al Hill. Ted was married but I don't think he had any children. Al was single, a young college student like me. Except Al was dead.

The memory of his torn and bullet-racked body came back to me strongly now and I could not help shaking and crying.

Late in the afternoon, we were put aboard a little narrow gauge railroad car with two guards and transferred up to Garmisch-Partenkirchen, a small city in the Alps where the 1936 Winter Olympics had been held. The Germans had long had a "ski troop" training base here for activities in Scandinavia and although their presence in the North had long ceased to be of any importance, they still maintained the training base.

I must digress a bit here. Forgive me if I have told this already, I can't remember. Back in 1937 or 1938, when I was 13 or 14 years old, the radio news was full of the impending crises in Europe and Asia and we all listened avidly to the news and read the *Abilene* [Texas] *Reporter/News* faithfully. One night, I had a dreadful nightmare wherein I was being chased by both Japanese and German soldiers atop a high wall overlooking a military compound high in the mountains. The details of the scene were etched vividly on my mind. I could see the camp very clearly and as the two troops closed in on me, I woke up screaming.

As we rounded a street corner in Garmish-Partenkirchen and were confronted with a view of the walled encampment, I had an overwhelming sense of *deja vu*, and when we entered the gates, I said to myself, "Shit. I've been here before!" It was exactly the place of my earlier dream from six years ago! I am not a strong believer in these types of phenomena, but the feelings were too strong to be disbelieved.

The eleven of us were held in the brig that night at Garmish-Partenkirchen. We spent an anxious and nearly sleepless night.

More later.
Skip

P.S. Bert was especially worried. Stories of the German's treatment of the Jews were already abounding and frightful. Bert was in the process of having his name legally changed to Lowell, but he was too late.

Chapter 10
In Captivity
"We were cursed, spat upon, hit and kicked..."

Manzanillo, Colima, Mexico
Martes, 28 de Feb 1989 [February 28, 1989]

Dear Heart,

When I started this tale, I had no idea or intention of making it so long, detailed, and drawn out. I hope I am not telling you "more than you wanted to know," like an engineer I once knew, who, if you asked him the time would tell you how to build a watch. But now that I am into it so far, I may as well continue.

In the brig at Garmish-Partenkirchen, they must have fed us that evening and the next morning, but I have no recollection of it. Sometime that morning, they put us on a train with two old guards bound for we knew not where. I don't remember any of that trip except for when we finally arrived at the main railroad station in Frankfurt and got off the train. Frankfurt was a major transportation center (among other things) and was one of the main targets of the 8th Air Force out of England. The rail yards and the station had been heavily, repeatedly bombed, both by the U.S. 8th Air Force and the RAF.

Nothing much of the station was left standing except the structural beams and the overhead girders. Nonetheless, the platforms were crowded with people, both military and civilians, waiting for trains that were still miraculously running. We had all doffed our fur-lined flying suits when we came down but were still in easily identifiable regalia: flight coveralls (with wings sewn on), flight jackets, etc.

Word spread quickly through the crowds that we were American "terror-fliegers" (terror bombers). We were cursed, spat upon, hit and kicked, while our two old guards made only half-hearted attempts to protect us from the mobs. The only thing that saved us from being strung up on the overhead girders was the fact that the makeup of the crowds kept changing as trains arrived and departed.

Finally, a little local two-car trolley-type train arrived and we were herded aboard it. After a relatively short ride, we arrived at a town on the outskirts of Frankfurt. I think it was Wetzlar, but I can't be sure. Here the Germans had a huge reception and interrogation center for incoming POWs.

Here we were put into small, individual rooms containing only a cot with a thin straw mattress, a chamber pot, a broom and a mop. There were no windows and the door was solid with a small peephole covered on the outside. There was a single, bare lightbulb suspended from the ceiling, but no switch.

Here I was left for several days. The guard would open the door in the morning with a cup of "coffee" and a piece of coarse, dark bread. I had to sweep and mop my room and empty the chamber pot in the latrine down at the end of the hall, accompanied by a guard. I saw no one else.

The light would go off and on erratically throughout the day and night. Occasionally during the day and night, a guard would noisily uncover the peep hole in the door and supposedly look in for several minutes. In the evening, he would bring a bowl of thin "soup" with another piece of the black bread.

Often and especially at night, there would be sounds of footsteps running in the hall and sounds of beatings and screams. This went on for so many days I lost count, never seeing anyone but a guard, looking forward every morning to the "coffee" and bread.

Absolutely nothing to do all day but sit on the cot and think, and dream, and remember better days, worrying about Mother and Sug and how they would react to the news from the 15th Air Force

Headquarters that I was missing in action and how long it would be before they learned I was OK and a POW in Germany.

When the guard would uncover the peephole, I would resolutely stare, unblinking, right at it until he let the cover drop again. I wondered about Dad, if he were still in England, and wondered where Lee was, and what duty he had finally drawn. (I hadn't heard from either of them while I was in Italy. Not their fault—mail was uncertain.)

As green and naive as I was, I realized this routine was a psychological softening up process but it went on long enough to begin to have an effect. But as scared as I was, I was absolutely determined that I would give only the information required by the Geneva Convention—name, rank and serial number.

Finally, when my interrogation began, it was almost anticlimactic. My first interrogator was a commissioned officer (as I think they all were), and I gave a proper salute, which he returned rather informally, and I stated my name, rank and serial number, stating further that under international law, that was all the information I was required to give him.

He smiled and said, "Sgt. Squyres, there is no need for such formality. Please sit down." Then he gave me an official International Red Cross form to fill out which of course included Mother's name and address for notification that I was a POW, but little else. [The War Department sent a telegraph to my grandmother on August 18, 1944, informing her that "your son, Staff Sergeant Weldon D. Squyres, has been reported missing in action since Three August over Germany." This was followed a few weeks later by another telegraph informing her, "Report just received through the International Red Cross states that your son, Staff Sergeant Weldon D. Squyres, is a prisoner of war of the German government."]

Then he told me that all my other crew members had been captured and were safe and unharmed, calling all of them by name and rank (except Ted and Al of course). I wondered how he knew the names of my crew members and asked him. He smiled an enigmatic little smile and said, "Sgt. Squyres, there are many, many things we know." I didn't realize until much later that I may have just given him confirmation that we were all of that crew. This went on for several days with different interrogators, some friendly, some tough and threatening.

But they *did* know far more about our operations of the 15th Air Force than *I* did, and I told them so. But in looking back, I'm sure they led me down the garden path, and I innocently corroborated some uncertain points for them and perhaps filled in some missing links in their knowledge.

They were very, very skillful at this and led you on so casually, telling you things they already knew that in spite of everyone's resolve (including mine) not to give any information. Out of the whole input, they were able to piece together a pretty accurate skein of information.

The most interesting to me was my last interrogation which wasn't an interrogation at all, but rather a lecture from a bright young officer on post-war developments in Europe. He very accurately predicted Soviet Russia's actions and role after the war, and their domination of Eastern Europe, and the tensions and friction between Russia and Western Europe and the United States. I was fascinated but unbelieving as Russia was then our staunch ally.

I never thought at the time to ask him why Hitler and Stalin had signed the non-aggression pact in 1940, which Hitler had then flagrantly violated when he later marched into Russia.

I wondered for a long time why I had been given this dissertation, and later decided it probably had been given to all POWs with some college education in the dim vague hope of Western post-war assistance to a defeated Germany against the mighty Russian Bear. Little did they know how woefully ignorant I was of world history, events and politics even though I had some college education.

Interrogations over at last, about six hundred of us were put on a train (boxcars this time) bound for a new Stalag-Luft at St. Wendell in the Saar Basin near Saarbrucken on the northern French border. I later realized these were the same boxcars the Germans used to transport to their deaths in other stalags and concentration camps the hapless Jews and other unfortunates who did not fit Hitler's Aryan mold. The trip was day-long and uncomfortable and the mid-August heat was suffocating. We were still strangers to one another, still unsure of our destinies, and mostly silent.

We were the first "kriegies" (*kreigsge-fangeners*—POWs) there. It was a small camp, the site had originally been horse stables for some large estate. Shelter was a long, tin-roofed area, completely open to the front with periodic separations along the length that had once been horse stalls.

Sleeping accommodations were wooden cots with a now familiar thin straw mattress. A makeshift kitchen occupied one end of the shed with a latrine at the other end. The whole area was fenced with barbed wire about twelve feet high and guard posts had been built all around the whole compound. According to the Geneva Convention, prisoners were separated by rank. Commissioned officers had their own camps. Non-coms had theirs. The poor damned infantry dog-face GIs, privates and PFCs had theirs.

The Germans, with their methodical logic, carried this even further—the camps were separated by branch of service. So all of us at St. Wendel were USAF non-coms and all our camps were Stalag-*Luft*- something. Luft meaning air as in the Luftwaffe, "air force." None of my non-com crew members were with me.

More later.
Skip

WESTERN UNION

1201

A. N. WILLIAMS
PRESIDENT

NEWCOMB CARLTON
CHAIRMAN OF THE BOARD

J. C. WILLEVER
FIRST VICE-PRESIDENT

The filing time shown in the date line on telegrams and day letters is STANDARD TIME at point of origin. Time of receipt is STANDARD TIME at point of destination

DA37 WM76

WMUF161 43 GOVT=WUX WASHINGTON DC 18 1132A

MRS VELMA C SQUYRES=

2512 29TH ST LUBBOCK TEX=

THE SECRETARY OF WAR DESIRES ME TO EXPRESS HIS DEEP REGRET
THAT YOUR SON STAFF SERGEANT WELDON D SQUYRES HAS BEEN
REPORTED MISSING IN ACTION SINCE THREE AUGUST OVER GERMANY
IF FURTHER DETAILS OR OTHER INFORMATION ARE RECEIVED YOU
WILL BE PROMPTLY NOTIFIED=

ULIO THE ADJUTANT GENERAL.

THE COMPANY WILL APPRECIATE SUGGESTIONS FROM ITS PATRONS CONCERNING ITS SERVICE

WESTERN UNION (30)

1201

A. N. WILLIAMS
PRESIDENT

The filing time shown in the date line on telegrams and day letters is STANDARD TIME at point of origin. Time of receipt is STANDARD TIME at point of destination

DAO WM58

WMUFOEPP 34 GOV=WUX WASHINGTON DC 5 829P SEP 5 PM 7 46

MRS VELMA C SQUYRES=

2512 29TH ST LUBBOCK TEX=

REPORT JUST RECEIVED THROUGH THE INTERNATIONAL RED CROSS STATES
THAT YOUR SON STAFF SERGEANT WELDON D SQUYRES IS A PRISONER OF
WAR OF THE GERMAN GOVERNMENT LETTER OF INFORMATION FOLLOWS FROM
PROVOST MARSHAL GENERAL=

J A ULIO THE ADJUTANT GENERAL.

THE COMPANY WILL APPRECIATE SUGGESTIONS FROM ITS PATRONS CONCERNING ITS SERVICE

Telegram dated August 18, 1944, informing his mother that
Weldon has been reported missing in action, and Telegram dated
September 5, 1944, informing his mother that
Weldon was a prisoner of war in Germany.

FIFTEENTH AIR FORCE
Office of the Commanding General
A. P. O. 520

12 September 1944

Mrs. Velma Squyres
2512 29th Street
Lubbock, Texas

My dear Mrs. Squyres:

I know that you must have been shocked by the report that
your son, Staff Sergeant Weldon D. Squyres, 38341514, is
missing in action and I wish that I might comfort you. As
much as I should like to do so I can give you no assurance
of his safety for my information is too incomplete.

Weldon was the radio operator on a Liberator which on
August 3, 1944, took part in a raid on an aircraft factory
at Friedrichshafen, Germany. While over Austria on the return from the target his ship was one of several that were
severely damaged in a battle with enemy fighters. Parachutes
were seen but it was difficult to tell from which plane they
came. Rest assured that you will be informed by the War Department as soon as we have any definite news of your son.

By his courage and devotion to duty Weldon won the respect
and admiration of all who knew him. The Air Medal which has
been awarded to him is a tribute to the splendid service he
has rendered his country in her hour of need. I share your
pride in his achievements and your hopes for his safe return.

Very sincerely yours,

N. F. TWINING
Major General, USA
Commanding

Letter dated September 12, 1944, from Major General
Twining of the 15th Air Force informing his mother that he
was missing in action over Germany.

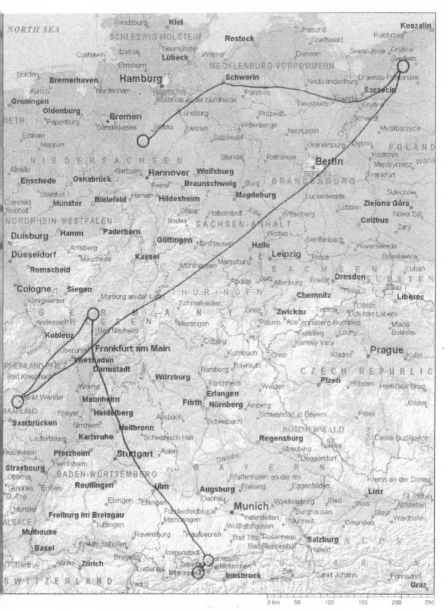

Map of the forced march across Germany
(credit and appreciation to Drew Squyres)

WESTERN UNION (41)

A. N. WILLIAMS
PRESIDENT

The filing time shown in the date line on telegrams and day letters is STANDARD TIME at point of origin. Time of receipt is STANDARD TIME at point of destination

DA48

D.WB695 48 GOVT=WASHINGTON DC 12 812P

MRS VELMA C SQUYRES=

2512 29 ST LUBBOCK TEX=

THE CHIEF OF STAFF OF THE ARMY DIRECTS ME TO INFORM YOU
YOUR SON STAFF SERGEANT WELDON D SQUYRES HAS RETURNED TO
MILITARY CONTROL AND IS BEING RETURNED TO THE UNITED
STATES WITHIN THE NEAR FUTURE AND WILL BE GIVEN AN
OPPORTUNITY TO COMMUNICATE WITH YOU UPON ARRIVAL=,
J A ULIO THE ADJUTANT GENERAL.

THE COMPANY WILL APPRECIATE SUGGESTIONS FROM ITS PATRONS CONCERNING ITS SERVICE

WESTERN UNION (36)

A. N. WILLIAMS
PRESIDENT

The filing time shown in the date line on telegrams and day letters is STANDARD TIME at point of origin. Time of receipt is STANDARD TIME at point of destination

DA36

D.WA959 22 TOUR=AREA 1 CAMPKILMER NJER 15 821P

MRS VELMA SQUYRES=

2512 29TH ST LUBBOCK TEX=

DEAR MOM AND FAMILY ARRIVED SAFELY WILL BE HOME SOON. DONT
TRY TO CONTACT ME UNTIL YOU HEAR FURTHER ALL MY LOVE=

SKIP.

THE COMPANY WILL APPRECIATE SUGGESTIONS FROM ITS PATRONS CONCERNING ITS SERVICE

Telegram dated May 12, 1945, informing his mother
that Weldon will be returned soon to the United States, and
Telegram dated May 15, 1945, from Skip (Weldon)
telling his mother he will be home soon.

Photo of Weldon D. Squyres in uniform
(appreciation to Katie Price for scanning)

The author and her uncle, Weldon Squyres, in Houston during
their last visit in September 1989.
Photo by the author's son, Ben Jordan.

The Prisoner of War Medal

The bronze medallion is 1-3/8ths inches in diameter. In the center is shown a bald eagle with its wings displayed. Forming a circle around the eagle and following the contour of the medal are barbed wire and bayonet points. The bald eagle represents the United States in general and the individual prisoner of war in particular. The eagle is standing "with pride and dignity, continually on the alert for the opportunity to seize hold of beloved freedom."

On the back is the inscription "Awarded to [name] for Honorable Service While a Prisoner of War." Following the curvature of the lower edge of the medal is inscribed "United States of America." Centered within the lower quarter of the medal is a crest taken from the Great Seal of the United States.

The ribbon consists of a wide central black band edged in white. Pinstripes of red, white and blue form the outer edge of the ribbon with red as the outermost color. The red/white/blue edge strips represent the United States. The larger white stripes represent hope, and the black center stripe symbolizes the bleakness of confinement as a prisoner of war.

The Prisoner of War Medal was established by Congress on November 14, 1986. It is awarded to any member of the Armed Forces who, since April 17, 1917, has been taken prisoner or held captive while engaged in an action against an enemy of the United States; while engaged in military operations involving conflict with an opposing foreign force; or while serving with friendly forces engaged in armed conflict against an opposing armed force in which the United States is not a belligerent party. The individual's conduct while in captivity must have been honorable.

The Prisoner of War Medal takes precedence by law after all unit awards and before all campaign and other service medals. It was designed by Jay C. Morris of the Army's Institute of Heraldry.

PRISONER OF WAR (POW) MEDAL APPLICATION/INFORMATION

(Please read Privacy Act Statement and instructions on reverse before completing form. All entries should be typed or printed. If more space is needed, continue in remarks block on reverse.)

Form Approved
OMB No. 0704-0288
Expires Jan 31, 1991

SECTION I - PRISONER OF WAR IDENTIFICATION DATA

1. NAME OF PRISONER OF WAR *(Last, First, Middle)*	2. SOCIAL SECURITY NUMBER	3. VA CLAIM NUMBER
4. SERVICE NUMBER	5. PLACE OF BIRTH	6. DATE OF BIRTH
7. BRANCH OF SERVICE	8. DATE CONFINED AS POW	9. UNIT OF ASSIGNMENT/ATTACHMENT WHEN CAPTURED
10. DATE RELEASED AS POW		

11. ADDITIONAL INFORMATION *(Place of imprisonment, disposition after release, or escape, recapture and release data)*

NOTE: PLEASE INCLUDE THE FOLLOWING DOCUMENTATION WITH APPLICATION

- If available, attach copies of WD AGO Form 53-55, DD Form 214, or other appropriate separation document issued at that time confirming POW Status
- If available, attach copies of documents specifying POW status, i.e., telegram notification to next of kin, POW identification card, newspaper articles

12. CURRENT STATUS *(X one)*				13. DATE OF RETIREMENT, DISCHARGE, OR DEATH
a. Reserve	b. Retired	c. Discharged	d. Deceased	

SECTION II - APPLICANT INFORMATION / FORWARDING INSTRUCTIONS

14 a. APPLICANT RELATIONSHIP TO POW *(X one)*	15. FORWARD POW MEDAL *(X one)*
(1) Same person identified in Section I	a. Directly to applicant *(Address shown in Item 14c)*
(2) Next of Kin *(Specify relationship)*	b. To the person / organization shown below who has agreed to receive and present medal *(Complete Item 16)* *(List Name, Organization, Street Number, City, State, and ZIP Code)*
(3) Surviving Spouse	
(4) Other *(Specify)*	
b. TYPED OR PRINTED NAME	
c. COMPLETE MAILING ADDRESS OF APPLICANT *(Please type or print)* *(List Name, Street Number, City, State, and ZIP Code)*	
d. TELEPHONE NUMBER *(Include Area Code)* e. DATE SIGNED	16. RELEASE AUTHORIZATION, IF REQUIRED
f. SIGNATURE	I hereby authorize release of the requested POW medal to the person/organization indicated in Block 15 b.
	(Veteran or Next of Kin Signature)

DD Form 2510, FEB 88

U.S. Government Form 2510—Prisoner of War (POW) Medal
Application/Information.

INSTRUCTIONS

- Use typewriter or print legibly all information when completing this form. Submit in original copy only. Complete all items. If the question is not appropriate, type or print "NONE." If requested information is unknown, type or print "UNKNOWN." Attach copies of all documentation available in support of your request.

- If space is insufficient, continue in block 17, "Remarks," below

- All applications for POW Medals MUST show Service Number if POW status existed prior to 1970.

- Veterans organizations, public officials, etc., are authorized to receive applications from eligible individuals or next of kin, forward them to the appropriate address listed below, and ask that medals be returned to them for subsequent presentation.

- For information on the POW Medal or to obtain copies of this form, you may call the following toll-free telephone number: 1-800-873-3768.

MAIL COMPLETED APPLICATION TO THE APPROPRIATE ADDRESS LISTED BELOW

ARMY	NAVY / MARINE CORPS / COAST GUARD	U.S. AIR FORCE (Including former Army Air Corps Personnel)
U.S. Army Reserve Personnel Center ATTN: DARP-PAS-EAW 9700 Page Boulevard St. Louis, Missouri 63132-5200	U.S. Navy Liaison Office National Personnel Records Center 9700 Page Boulevard St. Louis, Missouri 63132-5199	Air Force Reference Branch National Personnel Records Center 9700 Page Boulevard St. Louis, Missouri 63132-5199

17. REMARKS

Privacy Act Statement

AUTHORITY: 10 USC 1128; 44 USC 2907, 3101, and 3105; and EO 9397, November 1943 (SSN)

PRINCIPAL PURPOSE: To assist the facility servicing the records in locating those records and verifying entitlement to the POW Medal

ROUTINE USE: May be used by eligible individuals, their representatives, or next of kin to request issue of the POW Medal

DISCLOSURE: Voluntary, however, if the requested information is known and withheld, it may not be possible to determine an entitlement to the POW Medal

DD Form 2510 Reverse, FEB 88

☆ U.S.G.P.O. 1988 - 252-901/82639

Chapter 11
Birding, Fishing and Writing
"Weldon, did you know that there is a medal for former POWs?"

[Note: I mention in my following letter that Weldon was at the point of his narrative in recalling the milk-runs. Because of the two-week lag for mail in and out of Mexico, some of our letters overlapped and thus may sound out of sequence.]

Houston, Texas
March 6, 1989

Dear Weldon,

Please do not interpret my silence as lack of interest in your correspondence! I have been very busy since we got back from Matzatlan. I thought I wrote you a short note to tell you that we did not catch any fish much less *see* any fish, but had a good time anyway. I guess I didn't save my last letter to you on my computer because I can't find it, so forgive me if I repeat myself.

I have been very busy with my "part-time" job. Some weeks I put in over 40 hours on my job and you see why I put part-time in quotes. I was working on a project that awarded the National Space Trophy to Rear Admiral Richard Truly, a former astronaut and now Associate Administrator with NASA Headquarters in Washington [later Truly became the Administrator of NASA]. I won't go into detail on what all I did but it climaxed on February 2 at a news conference in downtown Houston that I was in charge of. It went very well. I even got a chance to tell Adm. Truly that if NASA decides to

90

send a writer into space on the Shuttle in order to relate the experience to the American people that I would go in a New York minute. [Note to NASA: This offer still stands!]

No one heard from me there for awhile. I called the grandparents on Jan. 20, their anniversary, and told Grandma then that they haven't heard from me because I had been working on a project that involved the National Space Trophy. To which Grandma replied (and you can just hear her), "Oh, Cindy Girl, I hope you get the trophy!" I didn't explain to Grandma, of course, that I wasn't qualified, but I did tell the people I work for that I had been nominated for the National Space Trophy by my grandmother.

She really made me feel good, and I realized that if I ever had low self-esteem or needed validation of self-worth, I could always call my Grandma!

Now I am working on another project and instead of explaining it, I'll just send this copy of a newspaper clipping that tells about it. I am really excited about writing the feature article for the 20th anniversary of the moon landing for *Aviation Week* and am researching the Apollo 11 lunar landing now. I will be working on the article with at least one other person and we had to show *Aviation Week* that we were writers, so I sent some old stuff and wrote a quick article about the aeronautics faction of NASA and how general aviation has benefited from the aeronautics research and development of NASA. I even talked with the editor of the local paper about being their aviation writer, but I don't have the word back from them on that yet. So this is what is keeping me busy now for the most part. I really enjoy what I'm doing, but I regret that it leaves me little time to do creative writing (science fiction) which is why I quit full-time work in the first place.

But back to Matzatlan. If I haven't told you, the highlight was the Mexican Fiesta at the hotel the last night we were there. They had a dancing horse, fighting chickens, machete dancers, and loads of drunken tourists all in the ballroom in true fiesta fashion. It was great. Overall, we found Mazatlan high-priced and past its former resort prime. I think our next trip to Mexico will be Cozumel sometime in

April. I will let you know.

I am delighted that you have taken an interest in bird-watching. Peterson wrote the bibles in bird watching. The book I have is *A Field Guide to Mexican Birds* by Peterson and Chalif. The anis look like black parrots with parrot-like bills. I never could identify the strange looking duck-like fowl on the Las Hadas golf course. They might be called coots. Let me know if you find out. In Yucatan I saw a pair of large blue birds, possibly a type of jay. Also lots of yellowish birds in the coconut trees that I couldn't identify (lots of yellow birds in bird book!).

I was really envious to hear of your sailfishing! Please send me the photo and I will return it to you. I haven't caught one yet, although I have videotape of a large sail we spotted from our boat and of another one that took the bait, but shook it out. I know they aren't edible, but aren't they exciting? I tried eating marlin while at Mazatlan (I will eat almost anything). It was very fishy, looked like salmon, and they prepared it sauteed with onions and green peppers with melted cheese on top. It is so strong, I couldn't eat it all. But at least I can say I have eaten marlin.

Speaking of marlin, remember the old Spencer Tracy movie *The Old Man and the Sea* where he played the Cuban fisherman? I haven't seen it in years, then it came on TV and I videotaped it to keep on the boat. Previously, I had tried for six months to locate it in video stores. The marlin sequence used in it was shot off the coast of Peru. I am looking into going to *Golfito Sailfish Rancho* in Costa Rica for fishing in both the Atlantic and Pacific.

I am going through your letters and no, you have not skipped anything or I would let you know. Your narrative is riveting and although you keep saying you can't remember details, I think you are being very informative with the details. Please keep it up.

I got a letter from Grandma and she says Granddad is doing better. Tomorrow is his birthday and he is saying that he is going-on-90, not that he is 89. I am sending him some bright spring flowers because the weather in Lubbock has been record-breaking cold lately.

I guess this is all the news I have for now. I will do better to keep in touch. Where you left off was after the mission you volunteered for and then all the milk-runs your regular crew ran.

Hope this finds you happy and well and Mexico sunny and warm!

Love,
Cindy

Houston, Texas
April 8, 1989

[I had read a magazine article about the POW medal which was established in 1985 for POWs in WWII, Korea and Vietnam. This made me wonder if Weldon knew about the medal and what he thought of it. So I asked him in this letter. This letter telling him I was saving his letters with his wartime "saga" crossed in the mail with his letter asking me if I had saved his letters.]

Dear Weldon,

You wrote that the "saga" was getting more difficult because after all this time, it was harder to remember the memories and details. And you were almost apologetic about it being so long and "drawn out." Please let me assure you, I am not finding your story the least bit overdrawn or boring. I am keeping all your letters in order not to lose any consistency. I have never heard of the "yellow noses."

I am keenly interested and amazed at your recall. I also think you should have been that writer you wanted to be at one time. Perhaps it is never too late to write. And as my favorite author, Robert A. Heinlein said, "Writing is a legal way of avoiding work without actually stealing and one that doesn't take any talent or training." I am presently attending a writer's seminar in the evenings and as the published writer who is heading this seminar said last Monday evening, "We are all misfits." I hope I am not being presumptuous by assuming that you might be interested in serious writing, but you certainly appear to me to have the knack for it. And besides, as you yourself said, you are an Anglo in Mexico speaking with a Portuguese accent. A true misfit! Ha!

I wanted to let you know, too, that we are tentatively planning a trip to the Manzanilla May 3-7. It is not definite yet, but knowing that it takes from 2-3 weeks for letters to get to you, I wanted to let you know. Should plans change at the last minute, I have your phone number. Here is the number at the villa for your information, 011—

—————————. We plan to have about 10-12 people with us and some of us want to charter a boat and fish, and we certainly want to see you and have you plan to join in all the fun. Shirley and Jim are looking for a place near us to move to and when they do, she will probably leave her current job, so this might be our last chance to stay at the corporate villa. Will keep you posted.

I finally got another set of pictures from last summer's reunion made for Grandma and Granddad. They called me last month on my birthday and both of them sounded great.

Weldon, did you know that there is a medal for former POWs? What are your thoughts about that?

There is going to be a 40th anniversary reunion in Frankfurt and West Berlin for all who participated in the Berlin Airlift on Sept. 24-Oct. 1. Wasn't Dad in on that for one flight?

Hope to keep hearing from you and to see you in about a month.

Love,
Cindy

Manzanillo, Colima, Mexico
Lunes, 10 de Abril 1989 [April 10, 1989]

Mi querida sobrina Cindy Lou,

Hola! Caro carazon, ¿Como está?

I returned to Mexico from California late (very late—plane was delayed four hours because of dense fog *here* at the airport: very unusual) Saturday night and after a lazy Mexican Sunday, meandered downtown this morning to pick up my accumulated mail. Was delighted of course to find yours of 6 March among the accumulation. I had been in California since 18 March, doing federal and state income taxes, and taking care of other business which wound up taking three weeks, so I did not take time to come back through Texas. I had originally planned to go to Lubbock, then maybe Houston for a day, but because I am in the midst of obtaining immigrant status here, I cannot be out of the country more than 30 days.

First, Dear Heart, there is never any need for apologies nor guilt feelings about time lapses in your correspondence to me. I know too well the pressures of time from work and study, and during the last several years of my working life I was the world's worst correspondent, relying on the phone instead. It is only since my retirement that I have started writing people again, and enjoying it, and now keep up correspondence with quite a few people—relatives and friends. Of course I *love* hearing from *you*, so don't get too engrossed in your work! Evidently, I have missed at least one of your letters—the last one received was the invitation to join you in Mazatlan for the fishing trip.

Your work sounds fascinating! Thanks for sending me the clip from the newspaper. Please keep me posted on what you are doing— are you still going to school? [I did not mention that in my letter, but yes, on top of everything, I was taking classes at the local college.]

I have long been a bird watcher and my books are all Peterson's. In January, I brought my *Field Guide to Western Birds* down with me and find that it augments Peterson and Chalif's Mexican bird book very well. Incidentally, I think the last time I wrote about birds, I was still in doubt about the identification of a wood ibis (or wood stork) and a whooping crane. Can now confirm he is a wood stork. The only other new species I have seen are white pelicans, which occasionally settle into the lagoons and marshes in large flocks. They are somewhat larger than the brown ones.

Your Las Hadas golf course bird is very likely a coot. There are hundreds of them in the lagoons and marshes. The thing that puzzles me though is that they mostly stay in or near to water. Don't know the Las Hadas area well, but assume there must be ponds or lagoons near the golf course.

I have sent pictures of my "pez vela" to many people and my memory tells me also to you but I can't be sure. Let me know if you did not receive it and I will certainly send you one. Did I tell you about the dolphins and the whales? I now write to so many people I can't remember what I have told to whom! I guess I should start some sort of diary or log.

I am glad you are enjoying my wartime chronicle. You should have received at least two more episodes since the one you mentioned, relating to the debacle of my first volunteer mission. I will resume the narrative in a few days—I have to get into a certain "mind set" before I can begin to dredge up those old memories. Incidentally, Cindy, this is the first time I have ever set this down on paper in some semblance of order, although I have related many of the events orally to my family and others. If you have kept them— and when I have completed it—would you make a copy of them and send to Lee? I will ask him to make copies for the rest of my family including perhaps Mom and Dad [my grandparents]. If you are interested, there are two excellent books you may want to read. One is *The Rise and Fall of the Third Reich* by William L. Shirer, the other a farcical but biting novel of life in the 15th Air Force called *Catch 22* by Joseph Heller.

I didn't see the movie *The Old Man and the Sea* but read the Hemingway book. To my mind, it's the best thing Hemingway ever did. Always thought he was overrated and thought John Steinbeck the far better writer. If you can find a copy, read his *Travels With Charlie*, a chronicle of a trip around the U.S. he took with his dog in a homemade pickup camper. It's poignant, sad, and hilarious. I've never gotten much into the science fiction genre—have read most of C.S. Lewis, some Asimov and Carl Sagan. Lewis was an English clergyman and there is always a theistic thread through his stories, but they were very good. I'm out of writing paper so will close for now. When you write your sibs and parents, give them all my love and regards. Also plan a fishing trip to Manzanillo! Can almost guarantee you a pez vela.

Much love,
Tio Skip

Chapter 12
The POW Medal
"No Dear Heart, I was not aware that such a thing existed, and at first it struck me as kind of funny..."

Manzanillo, Colima, Mexico
Thursday 21 April 1989

Dear Cindy Lou,

I received your very welcome letter of 8 April yesterday and am replying quickly in hope that you will receive this before you leave for Mexico. I do hope that "tentatively" will turn into a certainty. I will be delighted to see you all and maybe join in some of your festivities.

Thank you for your kind words about my writing—that's nice to hear coming from a pro! Yes, I have thought from time to time throughout my life about turning to writing, but I'm afraid it's now too late. I have sometimes wondered what my life would have been like if after the war I had returned to journalism instead of going into television engineering. But to coin a phrase, that's water over the dam and you can't live your life over (perhaps unfortunately!).

I cannot agree with your author Robert Heinlein about writing taking no talent and no training, and I'm sure he had his tongue firmly implanted in his cheek when he made the remark! (A difficult feat perhaps if he made it orally!) As you are well aware, writing does require talent, and a great deal of hard-required skills, patience, discipline and imagination. None of which I have, except maybe in the beginning, some talent. Another thing, I think, a good writer needs also to have been (or be) an omnivorous reader, which I have been all my life. I think you absorb elements of style and good composition almost by osmosis.

Heinlein's name rings a faint bell in my memory, but I can't recall any books of his I've read. As I think I've mentioned before, I haven't read much science fiction. If you think of it and have room in your bags, bring me one of his books. My favorite American author has always been John Steinbeck, and for just plain escape-type pleasure reading, John D. MacDonald. I think his Travis McGee series was great!

About the POW medal, no Dear Heart, I was not aware that such a thing existed, and at first it struck me as kind of funny; there is nothing very heroic about being taken prisoner, but maybe there is in surviving it! If you could look into it for me, I'm at least curious about it. I had an Air Medal, with at least one (and maybe two, I don't remember) Oak Leaf cluster, and two Presidential Unit Citations (for the 465th Heavy Bomber Group), for the two raids we did on Ploesti. But they, and a lot of my military records, were "gone with the wind" when the tornado hit Mother and Dad's house in 1970. [My grandparents' house was completely leveled in that great storm which killed nine people in Lubbock, many of whom were their neighbors. Grandma and Granddad were both injured; Granddad the most seriously with a punctured lung caused by fallen debris. Both fully recovered and rebuilt on the same site.] I could probably have had them replaced, but I never felt it was important.

Yes, your father flew the Berlin Airlift, as nearly as I can remember, from beginning to end, in C-47s and C-54. The one flight you may remember having heard about had nothing to do with the airlift, however. He was flying General Telford E. Taylor and his wife to Nuremberg in a DC-3. Taylor was a Judge-Advocate General Officer and was on his way to participate in the trials. The old "gooney bird" developed some kind of serious engine problems over Berlin, and Lec had the General and his wife bail out. I think Mrs. Taylor suffered a broken leg. Lec later landed the plane somewhere, safely. I'm a little surprised you don't know more about your Dad's military career—it was an exciting and important one, even though he never got overseas during the war. Did he never tell you kids anything about it? [Yes, but perhaps in the same vein as Weldon, he thought it was ancient history and spoke little of it. It was only when we kids had become adults did we fully realize the impact of World War II and our parents' contributions to the national effort.]

Will close for now and get this into the mail. I'm really looking forward to seeing you.

Love,
Tio Skip

Manzanillo, Colima, Mexico
3 de Mayo 1989

Dear Cindy Lou,

I was delighted to get your call Monday but very disappointed that your trip was postponed. I do hope you all can make it down here soon.

I don't really have any news this time, I'm just sending you a few pictures so you can have some idea of my place. *Not* the villa, but it suffices. Also a pic of the pez vela. I've made a few explanatory notes on the backs. Each time I go back to California, I'm sorely tempted to bring my Nikon F3 back with me (and my assortment of lenses), but I'm afraid of what the constant humidity may do to it and now if it happened to get stolen I could never replace it. So last X-mas Nikki gave me a little "point and shoot" 35 mm Kodak which I am (re)learning to use. It does pretty well, but is limited in what you can take by the very wide angle fixed lens. I think it's a 35 mm. I have a tendency not to get close enough to my subjects. I would like to take bird pics but can't do much with this little camera. I have a 70-200 mm zoom with the Nikon, and have taken a lot of good bird pics with it.

I am planning on coming back to Lubbock in late August to take the folks to the Cumbie family reunion, which is always on the Sunday before Labor Day, which I think this year puts it on September 3rd. I'm going by train—if my plans materialize. I've always wanted to travel this country by train and bus but have been a little afraid to get too far from my phone for very long in case of some emergency with Dad (or Mother). So this trip looks like a good way to do it—heading to Lubbock anyway. I go from here to Guadalajara (7 hours), stay overnight there. Next day to Mexico City—112 hours overnight in a Pullman compartment—then Mexico City to Nuevo Laredo (18 hours) also in a Pullman. Guess what the total fare is? $68.62!! With two nights in a sleeper! Isn't that fantastic? I will fly from Laredo to Lubbock—I assume for now that that is possible.

Anyway, I hope to see you on that trip. If you don't make the reunion, I will route myself back through Houston for a day or two if I can do that without upsetting your applecarts at the time.

That's all for now. I'll resume the war saga soon.

Much love to all,
Skip

Chapter 13
Camp St. Wendel
"...days of prison camp life, merging one into another with endless monotony and dreariness and hunger and cold and sickness..."

Manzanillo, Colima, Mexico
Domingo, 7 de Mayo 89

Dear Cindy Lou,

I know it has been awhile since I last wrote of this saga, and for some reasons unexplainable to myself, I have found it difficult to get psyched up for it to resume. One reason is that I really have better recall of my life in the service prior to "Kreigsgefangener" (POW) days, than I do of those.

Most of my life in the service was fun; even the physical rigors of basic training and gunnery school were no more rigorous than the hard physical labor I had done in my young life on farms and ranches. And I enjoyed being in good physical shape. Also, the schools' curricula were enjoyable. Radio school at Scott Field opened up an exciting new world to me of electronics and the things that could be done in communications. Gunnery school at Kingman was just plain fun, like being in a vast and varied shooting gallery with all the quarters in your pockets you needed. Learning the mechanical and physical properties of guns and ammo and ballistics was a wonderful extension of my boyhood pleasure in hunting rabbits, dove and quail.

Off-duty times were edenic [?]. The warm, wonderful support of the people for their "boys in uniform" made life off base a delight. During crew training at Westover (Mass.), Chatham (Ga.) and

104

Langley (Va.) proudly wearing sergeants stripes and crew member wings, we were treated as heroes without ever having fired a shot! And the pretty girls! It was hard not to fall in love at every place you were stationed!

To a naive, idealistic, romantic 18-19-year-old boy, whose horizons were bounded by where he had lived in West Texas and by what he had read, this was all pretty heady stuff and certain to make an impression on his memories. Even after going into combat, and coming face to face with the grim realities of real war—not a movie—of possible death, this new awakening to the realities of life and death also impresses itself onto your memory, and you do not ever really forget.

But the days of prison camp life, merging one into another with endless monotony and dreariness and hunger and cold and sickness, alternating at times with high hopes for rescue followed by endless despair—these days seem to get all rolled into one long period in which it is difficult to recall many details. But bear with me, I will do the best I can.

After the enforced and scary isolation of the interrogation center, it was a relief to be with fellow Americans, even as prisoners. We were hauled down to St. Wendel in the same boxcars the Germans used to haul hapless Jews, and unfortunate others who did not fit Hitler's Aryan model, to their deaths in concentration camps. I don't remember much about the trip except that it was crowded and uncomfortable and hot being mid-August. We were mostly strangers to one another and still cowed by our recent experiences. There was not much talk, mostly conjecture about where we might be going and what life was going to be like in camp. The trip did not take long, certainly not more than a day.

St. Wendel was a new camp, I don't remember the "Stalag-Luft" number. There were about 600 of us, all recently captured except for a small cadre of GI's from older camps who had been transferred to us to take over our organization in the new camp. Camp life was self-governed and these were guys with experience in what it was all about and what the Germans required. We were all assigned to different details on a rotating basis, mostly having to do with preparation and equal distribution of food and with general camp cleanliness.

We fell out in formation every morning and every evening for a head count about which the Germans were very rigorous with typical Teutonic thoroughness. They would count us over and over and recheck the numbers to make sure they complied with whomever might be excused from formation because of sickness, other duties, or whatever.

Apart from this, there was absolutely nothing to do except explore the small camp, perform your occasional small assigned camp duties, walk in the warm sun or loll in the shade. We began to become acquainted with one another and everyone soon came to know each other's war "horror stories." There were guys from both the 15th AF in Italy and the 8th AF in England and soon there were the inevitable and endless arguments about who had the toughest war and about the relative merits of the B-24 versus the B-17.

None of my other enlisted crew members were in this camp, and I soon found this to be true of most of the others. Whether this was by coincidence or Germanic design, I never knew. In keeping with their Teutonic nature, the Germans were very punctilious in the organization of prison camps. Commissioned officers had their own camps. NCOs also had their own. This was further broken down by branch of service. Thus, all Air Corps people were in "Stalag-Lufts." All ground force personnel were in Stalags (as in Stalag 17, if you saw that movie). I don't know how much further they carried this organizational neatness but anyway, those of us at St. Wendel started out mostly as strangers to one another. This passion for organization and detailed record keeping led to their undoing after the war for they had kept meticulous, detailed records of every human atrocity they committed, including wholesale destruction of the Jews!

Germany had thousands—even millions of Russian POWs. Since Russia was not a signatory to the Geneva Conventions, they used the Russian POWs as slave labor. We watched them from camp as they dug trenches and built tank traps in the woods surrounding our camp.

In the distance, we began to hear the rumble of heavy artillery fire that grew slowly closer, day by day. New incoming POWs brought word that General George Patton's Third Army was making a rapid advance through France toward southern Germany's Saar Valley. As the sounds of gunfire drew closer, hope and optimism soared that we would soon be free.

I don't remember a whole lot more about life at St. Wendel. I don't remember what we had to eat, although it must have been adequate, as I have no memory of having been particularly hungry there! I only remember the rising expectations of being freed by Patton's Third Army and the desolation of the morning in mid-September at morning head count when we were informed that the entire camp would be evacuated the following day and to prepare for such evacuation. Quickly-formed small groups met to discuss ways and means of circumventing the evacuation and either trying to make way through the lines to Patton's troops or to hole up until Patton overtook the area. No one could come up with a single plan that did not mean almost certain death.

Your loving unc,
Skip

Chapter 14
Night of Terror
"We cowered in fear...listening to the bombs exploding...not relishing the bitter irony of being done in by our Allies."

Manzanillo, Colima, Mexico
11 de Mayo 1989

Querida Cindy Lou,

I ended my last report, if memory serves correctly, on a rather dramatic note which I now feel I must put into a more realistic perspective.

First of all, I said that the Germans made the announcement of the next day's evacuation at the *morning* body count. I really don't remember, but it must have been at the *evening* body count. They surely would not have given us that much notice. That would have left us much less time to make any "plans."

Second, I mentioned that there were many "meetings" about how we might circumvent this evacuation, and either stay in place or hole up somewhere and successfully wait out the arrival of Patton's Third Army. There were no structured "meetings" or any real "plans" discussed, there were just a lot of bitter mutterings and idle threats in a gloomy aura of disappointment and despair.

It was mid-September. Most of us had been prisoner a little more than month and we had built high hopes for a quick liberation by Patton as the sounds of the heavy artillery drew nearer. But unarmed, dressed in prison garb with a large black K printed on the back of our tunic, not speaking German and not knowing the geography of the area, it would have been sheer folly to have attempted an escape. The German army was still fighting fiercely and retreating slowly, and to have been out on one's own and get caught up in that retreat would have been almost certain death, even if one could have somehow successfully eluded the guards and the dogs.

So, on an early mid-September morning after a rigorous head count, we were marched in small formations back to the St. Wendel train yards accompanied by plenty of guards and dogs and loaded on to the "luxury" boxcars. Again, I don't remember many details of this trip except for seven or eight days and nights of misery, hunger, and sheer physical discomfort.

One detail does remain in memory—a night of terror in Berlin's rail yards undergoing heavy bombardment by the RAF's night bombers. Disruption of Germany's transportation system was a high Allied priority and major rail yards such as Berlin and Frankfurt were prime targets, regularly hit. So we cowered in fear that night, listening to the bombs exploding, some very close, sure that we had "bought the farm" and not relishing the bitter irony of being done in by our Allies.

A huge ack-ack gun was mounted on a flat car near our box car and each time it fired, the repercussions seemed almost certain to blow our car off the tracks. British Spitfires [fighter planes] based in France, were strafing the yards and the sounds were terrifying, sometimes too close. German fighters were in the air, some engaging the bombers, some dueling the Spits.

We could hear it all—the British Lancasters [bombers] didn't fly as high as we did in our Liberators, especially on night missions. It was a living nightmare out of Dante's *Inferno*, and there were a lot of tight sphincter muscles and Hail Marys that night.

Daylight finally came and the paralyzing fear slowly relaxed. Incredibly, miraculously, our train had not been hit. After almost a full day of backing and hauling, switching tracks and waiting for repairs to be made, we chugged slowly out of Berlin with a great deal of relief.

We had been heading generally northeast since leaving St.

Wendel and continued in that direction. We took turns standing at the small openings in the upper walls of the car, noting the names of the cities and towns we passed through. We knew enough of German geography through previous map study to have a pretty good idea of where we were, but not where we were going.

Accommodations on the train were not first class. The latrine was several buckets in each car emptied by the guards when we stopped. Breakfast was ersatz coffee and a piece of course black bread smeared with a little rancid butter or some jam (but never both). Dinner (lunch was omitted) was a thin soup, usually potatoes or kohlrabis, sometimes with little chunks of questionable meat— although we didn't question it. We did what exercises we could in the crowded conditions to ease cramped and aching muscles. Our toilettes were done with buckets of fresh water supplied each morning—we all suspected that the buckets were the same ones used as the latrines, but tried to think not.

Thus did our sight-seeing trip through Germany go, for seven or eight days. We finally arrived at a desolate little village called Kiefheide, in what had been eastern Poland before the Nazi occupation only a few kilometers from the Baltic coast. Gratefully we de-trained and marched in ragged formation about 4 kilometers down a narrow dirt road on aching, protesting muscles, tired, hungry, weak—but glad to be alive and in the open—to huge, sprawling Stalag Luft 6.

More later,
Love, Skip

Chapter 15
Life in the Stalag
"We were always hungry...I traded my senior high school class ring to a guard for a can of sugar."

Manzanillo, Colima, Mexico
Domingo 14 de Mayo 1989

Dear Heart,

I *think* it was Stalag Luft 6, I can't remember for sure. Anyway, it doesn't really matter. It is difficult to try to describe it to you, it seemed so vast after the small, raw, new compound at St. Wendel. If you saw (and remember) the old POW movie from several years back, *Stalag 17*—it was much like that. Incidentally, that movie was the most realistic POW movie I saw in later years, although I didn't go to many of them.

There were four separate large compounds at Stalag-Luft 6, each separated from the other, but all connected to a central area which comprised the German camp command area. Each compound was surrounded by the standard high barbed-wire fence, electrified, with higher machine gun-manned towers equipped with flood lights at regular intervals. Inside the fence in each compound, about 50 yards from the fence and about three feet high, ran a "warning wire." You could not cross that warning wire without immediately being machine gunned from the nearest tower.

Inside each compound was a series of long, low barracks, about two or three deep, that housed the prisoners. In the open area of the compound formed by the fences and barracks, and toward the entrance to the German headquarters, was a large building which housed the compound's kitchen, the Yanks' administrative headquarters, a small library and dayroom and a sick bay. Considerably farther down into the compound from that was a large central latrine with its own septic tank.

In the front end of each barracks there was also a latrine area which also served as the place for bucket showers and the daily morning toilette. So, consider a large (very large) fenced in area with barracks in tiers, two or three deep (I don't remember) situated around the perimeter, well removed from the warning wire, a headquarters building at the end leading into a camp headquarters and a latrine in the center fairly distanced away. That leaves a large amount of space in the center and around the perimeter of the fences away from the warning wire for physical activities, mostly walking. Each barracks housed about 200 prisoners divided into four rooms on each side of a long central aisle. Beds were piles of loose straw over which a blanket was tucked with another blanket for cover.

Stalag-Luft 6 was an old, well-established encampment, well organized and run by U.S. airmen who had been among the first U.S. prisoners taken by the Germans. It was a relief for me to be in a more structured setting after capture, interrogation, isolation, and the unsettling times at St. Wendel.

Us newcomers were assigned in a more or less random manner, among the four compounds. I asked around about my other crew members and after a while discovered that Bob Salmon was in one of the other compounds. I never had any word about the others, although I did see Nate Evetts in Slaton, Texas, after the war.

I put in a request to be transferred to Bob's compound but the Germans refused (no reason, just company policy!) We met from time to time at the warning wires of our respective compounds, but it is difficult to hold much conversation across 100 yards. Bob had landed hard due to a more rapid than normal descent because of the holes burned in his chute, but was not too badly hurt. He had managed to hide out in the mountains for a couple of days before capture, living on the emergency K-rations in his escape kit and with water from a mountain stream.

The days began to settle into a routine. Being so far north and so close to the Baltic, the late September days were crisp and quite pleasant. (We would later long for some summer warmth.) After breakfast and morning head count, we spent most of the day outside in the sun, walking the rounds of the compound or playing baseball or tossing a football. The International Red Cross from Switzerland had furnished some sports equipment, baseballs, bats, and gloves, and a few footballs to the camp. There were also a few ragged, tattered books in the dayroom "library." After evening headcount and chow, we were locked in the barracks, and guards and dogs patrolled the compound, floodlighted by the rotating beacons in the towers. Evening activities in the barracks consisted of card games— bridge mostly and pinochle, and when we had cigarettes, poker. There was also the inevitable and eternal internecine warfare (mostly good natured) between the members of the 8th and 15th Air Forces and the competing virtues of the Fort and the Lib. I sometimes wished the Germans had carried their Teutonic methodology even further and segregated their Kriegies by Air Force!

The favorite topic of conversation was food. Everyone rhapsodized about favorite dishes, and mom's (or wives') cooking, and about how when we get out, the first thing I'm gonna do is have a dozen hamburgers, or this or that. For the married guys and those with girlfriends, this was the second thing they were gonna do!

Food was a constant preoccupation. We were always hungry. Breakfast was always the ersatz coffee and black bread, with either butter or jam, or sometimes with a little smearkase, a kind of cheese. There was no lunch. Supper was almost always potato or kohlrabi soup, sometimes with a little meat in it, sometimes with a little black bread. (A kohlrabi is a variety of turnip.) From time to time, usually about once a month, we would get—Heavenly days!—Red Cross parcels. A Red Cross parcel was designed to provide one person with the minimum caloric intake for one week. The contents varied from parcel to parcel but always included a can of powered whole milk (Klim), two heavily hard, concentrated sweetened chocolate bars

(D-bars) and four packs of cigarettes. The variations would be either a package of (great, wonderful) hard yellow cheese or a tin of corned beef or Spam (love it!). One Red Cross parcel was apportioned to four people and was divided up very meticulously. The D-bars and the cigarettes became currency between ourselves and with the guards.

The compound was a microcosm study in economics. When the parcels first arrived, inflation became rampant. It took a whole pack of cigarettes to buy what three weeks later could be bought for one cigarette. The guards prized the American cigarettes and would trade fresh potatoes, kohlrabis, cheese, sausage, sugar or whatever, at whatever the going rate was at the time. The rate, of course, depended on how long it had been since the last parcels had arrived. The D-bars were also valuable currency, but cigarettes became the gold standard. Between ourselves, they became poker chips with the value fluctuating with the inflation rate. Those who did not smoke made out the best by hoarding their cigs during periods of high inflation until they were worth much more.

I had started smoking a pipe when I was at Tech—I thought it made me look older and gave me a sort of "Joe Cool" image. It had become a fixed habit and when I was shot down, I had a pipe and a full pouch of tobacco in my pockets which the Germans let me keep. When I had finally depleted my tobacco pouch, I started crumbling cigarettes into my pipe and rationing myself carefully, but the nicotine habit had me in its grip and in the worst of all possible circumstances—burning up GOLD. I became a cigarette smoker.

With the arrival of parcels, our rooms in the barracks became a gourmet kitchen. We had a small coke-fired stove in each room and a ration of coke made from coal dust and God only knows what else. This was for heating during the winter but with potatoes and onions purchased from the guards and tins of corned beef from the parcels, we made delicious corned beef hash. With kohlrabis, Spam and other assorted ingredients, a heavenly stew. Shaved D-bars mixed with Klim and a little black bread and a little water made wonderful desserts. Ah, that was life! There just wasn't enough of it.

You must cast your mind's eye back into history a bit. In the late 1930s and early '40s, life in the U.S. was very provincial. Air travel as we know it today did not exist. Major modes of transportation were by rail and bus and that, except for local travel, was only for the wealthy. Thus we had a very limited view of the world.

When the Japanese attacked Pearl Harbor, most Americans did not know where the hell Pearl Harbor was! Hawaii at that time was a little known territory of the U.S., except for a fortunate few who had been there on holidays!

Thus we were the products of our own upbringing and had little in common except the desire to perpetuate the "American way of life" as we individually knew it. For Texans and most southwesterners, this was a traditional Anglo-Saxon view. We knew American history, we had read it, and studied it, but we had not experienced it firsthand. Ours was a long heritage dating back to the revolution, and later, the Alamo. We did not fully grasp what America meant to the later arriving Irish, Swedes, Poles, Greeks, Hungarians, Jews, and even the Mexicans. As southwesterners, our experience with the "Mescans" had mostly been with the Indian peon class, and we tended to slur over the fact that several of the defenders in the Alamo had been Mexicans.

So the democracy of the armed forces had finally brought us all together and in no circumstances more intimately than in a POW camp. For me, it was an enlightening and educational experience. There was Adam "Polack" Polansky—an early Polish emigre to New York who went to all the utility companies in New York to pay his gas, electric and phone bills because on all the walls in New York City were signs saying "Post No Bills."

There was Hank Sytnik, another Polack who had no nickname— Hank was enough. He gave me personal instructions in the rites of the Catholic Church. I had met and fallen in love with a young Polish-American girl in Westover, Mass., and was seriously considering becoming Catholic in order to ask her to marry me.

There was "Frenchy" Lavoisier from Maine—one of the many French descendents of those who had settled in the northern U.S. and

Canada, and whose ancestors had fought with Lafayette for the Yanks in the Revolutionary War.

There was "Hunky" Jim Veres—a several generations removed Hungarian who was a good friend of mine and who later became a Lt. detective on the Cleveland police force. There was Jose Quinones, the "Prune Picker" from Los Angeles, who was a student at UCLA. There were "Swedes" and "Greeks" and what have you. None of these appellations had any perjorative content, they were given in the same sense that I was often called "Tex."

Thus did pass the days of September and October 1944. We had high hopes of being home by Christmas.

Someone in one of the other compounds somehow had access to a short wave radio—I never knew how—probably heavily bribed a guard somehow. But anyway, he got the BBC [British Broadcasting Corporation] news and would circulate it every day or so to the other compounds by runners who reported to each barracks. We also got news from new incoming prisoners and the Allied offenses were going well on all fronts. The Russians were advancing westward along the Baltic Coast and had taken the port city of Danzig (now called Gdansk).

In November, it turned extremely cold with snow and we spent most of the days inside huddled around our little stove, carefully husbanding our little ration of coke. During the evening headcounts, we could see the contrails of the V-2 rockets blasting off from Peenemunde and Schweinewundi to the west heading towards London. These were Hitler's vaunted "secret weapon," courtesy of Dr. von Braun and his Black Forest elves.

In December, we got the distressing news of the German breakthrough in the Battle of the Bulge and gave up all hope of being home by Christmas.

I have absolutely no memory of that Christmas or New Year except for being cold, hungry, and miserable.

More later.
Much love,
Skip

Chapter 16
The Forced March, Escape and Freedom
"We contacted dysentery, and shit and died our way across Germany...bedlam erupted inside the camp...we tore down the guard towers and made bonfires..."

Manazanillo, Colima, Mexico
Jueves, 18 de May 1989

Querida Sobrina,

In early January 1945, the rumble of heavy artillery could be heard to the east, growing a little louder each day, rekindling hope of liberation by the Russkies. The Russian prisoners, kept in a separate compound for coolie-type camp labor (cleaning the septic tanks with their "super duper pooper scooper" for instance) became noticeably more excited and elated each day. When they were in our compound and we were around watching them work, they would grin slyly and rub their nose or cheek and very surreptitiously make Churchill's V for Victory sign. They had to be very careful doing this, for, if a guard caught one, they would literally beat the shit out of the poor booger.

We were not allowed to fraternize in any way, although I don't know if anyone in our group spoke any of the Russian dialects, but anyway, the guards didn't even like us hanging around where they were working, and would soon chase us off with their dogs.

One rare, bright sunny day in January, most of us were out, making the rounds of the warning wire and enjoying the sun's relative warmth. Suddenly, from the east at a very low altitude, two FW 190's zoomed over our camp doing snap rolls. Evidently they were returning from a successful mission at the eastern fronts and celebrating.

Suddenly, for some reason we never learned, one of the pilots lost control of his plane and he plowed into the ground in the woods near the camp in a tremendously loud burst of smoke and flame. There was a hushed silence and then a loud spontaneous cheer arose from all the compounds.

It seemed as if it were some kind of good omen. I don't know if orders were given, but the tower guards suddenly began raking the compounds with machine gun fire and we made panicked dashes to the nearest barracks and very quickly the compounds cleared. We were stunned and shaken by the suddenness with which everything had happened, and we remained inside, cowed, for the rest of the day until evening head count.

The bitter winter cold returned, and we were once again, cold and hungry. The entire German infrastructure was breaking down and we had no Red Cross parcels for a long time. The German port of Lubeck [ironically, similar in sound to Lubbock, Texas] where the parcels arrive, had been heavily bombed, and what rail transportation that still existed was devoted to troop movements.

I traded my senior high school class ring to a guard for a Klim can full of sugar.

We formed combines of two or three or sometimes four to pool mutual resources. I teamed up with "Kohlrabi" John Frawley from Ithaca, NY, "high above Cayuga's waters," home of Cornell University, and Bob Sage, another NY up-stater whose major contribution was a sly, droll grin with which he could find humor in the most ludicrous situations. A laugh was as necessary to survival as a slice of black bread.

The German breakthrough in the Battle of the Bulge [December 1944] had been contained and Hitler's desperate, last gasp attempt to regain the offensive had failed. The war ground on and on to its inexorable conclusion, but still the Germans fought on desperately. Our morale increased as the Eastern front artillery fire became louder and louder, and served to sustain us in spite of the hunger. Hope, as well as humor, can be the equal of a fresh kohlrabi or a couple of small potatoes in sustaining life.

One morning in late January at morning head count, we were instructed to return to barracks, assemble our blankets and all personal gear (ha) and regroup in the compound in thirty minutes.

Our hearts sank as we realized this was to be another evacuation. But barracks by barracks, compound by compound, we formed up [approximately 10,000 prisoners] and marched raggedly out the gates and onto the little road to Kiefheide, not dusty now, but covered with hard packed snow.

When we reached Kiefheide, we kept going. This time there was not to be the "luxury" of our boxcars! This time it was to be a long, cold, dreary, hungry, killing (literally) march of some 300 miles across northern Germany in the dead of winter to an unknown destination. It took all that day and I think part of the next, to completely evacuate the camp and get approximately 10 thousand Kriegies strung out on the road. We were accompanied by guards and dogs, and at intervals, wagons drawn by oxen which carried food supplies and served as the soup kitchen. That first day our group only made about twelve to fifteen miles and flopped wearily in a barn filled with straw, after the evening head count and a half Klim can of soup.

Next morning after head count, ersatz coffee and black bread, we hit the road again with tight, stiff, sore, aching, protesting muscles. The future looked very bleak again.

More later.

Love,
Skip

Manzanillo, Colima, Mexico
Sabado, 20 de Mayo, 1989

Querida Cindy Lou,

We marched—plodded, trudged, staggered are better words—
ever westward through frozen rain, through sleet, and through snow,
sleeping sometimes in barns, and sometimes in open fields in rain
and snow. We kept to country roads through small villages to keep
from obstructing the military flow on main thoroughfares.
Everywhere we saw evidences of the collapse of the German
infrastructure.

We saw ME 109s riding piggy-back on the backs of Junkers and
Heinkel HE-111 bombers headed toward the Russian front to
conserve fuel. We saw trucks with small boilers heated by wood and
coke converted to steam power, also to conserve fuel. Occasionally
we saw in the air—very impressive—the ME-210, twin engine jet
fighter plane, another of Hitler's secret weapons, and more effective
than the "buzz bombs," the V-2 rockets. These ME-210s were the
first jets (pure jets, not propjets) and, although coming too late in the
war to be truly decisive, were more effective in their effort than the
V-2 rockets.

We also saw hundreds and thousands of German civilians on the
roads, on foot, in oxcarts and wagons, fleeing the Russian juggernaut
coming from the East. It was a time of almost utter chaos and very
dangerous. It was very tempting to make an escape attempt and many
were made, and many were shot.

Early on, Kohlrabi John, Bob Sage and I held a council of war and
concluded that to make an escape attempt under the circumstances
would be the height of foolhardiness and that our best bet would be
to continue as we were—to somehow survive until the inevitable end
of the war. That we pledged ourselves to do.

We suffered the cold, and the wet, and slept—or tried to, in open
fields where we could not light fires because of the RAF night
bombers. Those of us from St. Wendel remembered our night in the

Berlin rail yards and cursed the RAF.

Passing through villages, we drank from the village pump, and washed ourselves as best we could and cleaned our Klim can mess kits. We contracted dysentery and shit, and died our way across Germany. We suffered frozen feet, and ears, and hands and those who fell by the wayside were set upon by dogs, driven until they could go no further, and then left to die by the side of the road. Some of the kinder guards—old-timers, mostly WWI retreads—would put as many as could be accommodated on the supply wagons. There they would be laid over with supplies (to hide from the other guards) until circulation was cut off in their legs, and they would develop gangrene and die.

Dysentery was the worst and most often fatal problem. We were all affected by it. How some of us got through and some didn't, I still don't know. I think it had to do, somehow, with a determination to survive. Kohlrabi John, Bob Sage and I had that determination and somehow reinforced it in each other. During rest stops, we, along with the others, would scour the surrounding fields, digging for overlooked potatoes or kohlrabis from the preceding harvest. It was surprising how many you could find!

One night in a barn when things looked darkest, Kohlrabi John revealed to Sage and I that he had saved a pack of cigarettes (he didn't smoke) from the last Red Cross parcels at Keifheide. He had a hunch that it might be a lifesaver some time in the future! He thought now that the time had finally come to use it. With typical sly, cunning Yankee ingenuity, Kohlrabi John very carefully undid the cellophane wrap at the bottom of the package, then, just as carefully, undid the package itself at the bottom, and removed the twenty cigarettes.

He then refilled the package with carefully broken bits of straw so that it perfectly resembled a full package of cigarettes. With a small, carefully hoarded bit of Klim and a bit of spit, he resealed the package and the cellophane wrap and—*voila*—we had a package of straw that looked exactly like a package of American cigarettes. It fell to Bob Sage's lot, with his old Yankee spieler's talent, to peddle them. Using the standard call, "Posten! Posten! Mus scheissen!" (Guard! Guard! I have to take a shit!), he wandered out as far as he dared from where we were, and engaged a perimeter guard in trade conversation. He wound up trading the straw cigarettes for a good quantity of cheese and sausage, then beat a hasty retreat to our position where we hid him, the cheese and sausage under the straw.

Soon the camp was in an uproar with the outraged guard looking for the transgressor, but of course he never found him. The unfortunate guard could not make a complaint to his superior because it was "verbotten" to trade with the krigesgefangeners. We used the 20 cigarettes in the following days to trade among the kriegies because we didn't dare make offers of single cigarettes to the guards! Thus we bought a few extra days of life.

After several weeks on the road, the march began to split up, some groups taking one turn of the road, some another. Our group kept heading generally due west and in mid- to late March, we arrived at a little town called Fallingboestel, situated almost in the center of a triangle formed by Hamburg, Hanover and Bremen, not far from the North Sea.

Outside the town was a huge POW camp, larger than the little city itself. It was filled with Brits and Frenchmen who had been prisoners since 1940 when France fell and the Germans had repulsed the first British invasion forces at Dunkirk.

Here we were distributed among the various British compounds. Bob, Kohlrabi John and I managed to stay together and the Brits kindly made room for us, got us beds with fresh straw and blankets and shared their rations. This camp appeared to be relatively well fed and the German discipline was much more lax than what we had been used to. Still, there was the morning and evening head counts and the Americans were counted separately.

We thought we would end the war here, but in a few days the guards began falling the Americans out in small groups and marching out the gates, going God only knew where.

We later heard one horror story of what happened to one group of about one hundred men. They were sleeping in a barn one night when a roving band of SS troops [elite and feared Nazi soldiers] took over from their guards, set fire to the barn, then machine gunned them down as they tried to flee the burning barn.

The American exodus continued with two or three small groups leaving each day. We three musketeers held another powwow and decided we were going to stay! The Germans kept track of us only by numbers, and we managed to be scarce when the calls came to fall out.

When the last group of Americans left, the Germans knew they were three prisoners short and a search of the compound was made. The Brits had hidden us in the loft of a small chapel and managed in various ways to divert the searching guards away from the chapel. The old guards didn't have much heart in the search anyway and after a couple of days, it was abandoned.

The Brits who had been sneaking us food and water told us they thought it was safe to come down and we did. One by one at intervals we quietly joined the various groups of Brits who loitered casually around the chapel. We had "escaped" inside a German POW camp!

We managed to avoid the British head counts in various ways, so the Germans wouldn't wonder all of a sudden how they had come up with three extra Brits!!

In early April, the sounds of war again came closer, this time from the west and in the late afternoon of April 15th, there was a fierce battle fought around Fallingboestal and we saw German troops and tanks retreating. On the morning of April 16, 1945, there were no whistles, no shouts of "rausmitt, rausmitt," no "mach schnell, mach schnell" for the morning head count.

We got up to find the camp completely deserted by Germans—the guard towers were empty—no guards or dogs in the compound!

We all gathered by the warning wires, wondering what to do—too frightened and unbelieving to do anything. Soon we heard the sounds of approaching tanks and then they hove into view, clattering by the fence with British Tommies throwing round loaves of crusty *white* bread and tins of meat over the fence!

It was the British 8th Army under General "Monty" Montgomery

AND WE WERE FREE!!

Bedlam erupted inside the camp. There was shouting and laughter and crying and dancing. We tore down the warning wire and tore down the fences and gates. We tore down the guard towers and made bonfires and feasted on the bread and meat not worrying about saving part of it. We went into Fallingboestal—deserted—raided cellars, found eggs, stole chickens, ducks and geese. We did not break into houses. Monty had left troops in the town to keep some semblance of order but our bounty was enough. That night we had fresh eggs, and chicken, ducks and roast goose, and wine and schnapps.

The Russian slaves joined us and got drunk, and we sang and did Cossack dances together until we fell down. It was a glorious day and night!

Early the next morning, a long string of British lorries arrived with a cadre of officers and men to oversee the evacuation. Somewhat surprised to find three stray Yanks in the ranks, the British authorities put us on high priority and Kohlrabi John, Bob Sage and I were among the first to leave.

They trucked us several miles to an airstrip with waiting DC-3s and flew us to Brussels, then to the British garrison headquarters. They showered us, de-loused us, and examined us. I weighed in at 117 lbs., down somewhat from my normal 158 to 160 lbs. They issued us clean underwear and British Tommy uniforms complete with brown berets and black boots. They advanced us $100 U.S. in Belgian francs and told us to go see the city and return to the garrison that evening.

We strolled all over downtown Brussels in a daze, scarcely believing we were alive, thinking we had died and gone to heaven. We returned to the garrison that evening in time for evening chow and were billeted to fresh, clean comfortable beds—with real sheets. The next morning they put us on a train with proper travel credentials bound for La Harvre, France, where the U.S. Army had a huge debarkation center, Camp Lucky Strike.

What a glorious train ride and how different from our last one. Is it any wonder I've always loved the Brits!

We three would look at each other and just grin, without saying anything. We all thought we looked pretty sharp in our Brit uniforms with the berets cocked at a jaunty angle!

After a few days of processing at Camp Lucky Strike, we boarded a ship in La Harvre Harbor. I don't remember the name of it— President Something—but it had been an old luxury liner now converted to a troop ship. President Wilson had sailed on that ship to Europe in 1919 to sign the Treaty of Versailles ending World War I.

Now it was filled to the gunwales with the "sick, lame and lazy" liberated POWs, wounded, and those sick in mind or body. There were also two USO show troupes aboard who put on shows every night. I don't remember much about that trip except that I loved it!

I don't remember our departure date but we were escorted by two destroyers as the war was still on and German U-boats were still active in the Atlantic. I spent most of the days on the top deck, on the bow, watching the bow wave and helping the destroyers watch for periscopes!

We were about in mid-Atlantic when news came of the German surrender [May 7, 1945]. The ship became a joyous place.

We were all on deck when we steamed into New York Harbor, and we hugged and shouted and pounded each other on the back and cried when we passed by the Statue of Liberty.

We were accompanied by fireboats spouting streams of water, with sirens wailing, and by a flotilla of tug boats and other boats, all tooting whistles, and bells and foghorns. When we finally docked, there was a huge crowd of cheering, screaming people, and as we debarked, the dear old Red Cross was there handing out paper cups of hot cocoa and cookies.

They must have wondered what three British Tommies were doing on this shipload of homecoming Yanks! We boarded a train at dockside for a quick trip across the river to Fort Dix, New Jersey. For chow that evening we had big, thick, juicy steaks that almost overlapped the mess tray. It was a kriegie's dream come true.

The next day we were given two free long-distance phone calls and I called home and talked to Mother and Dad, and told them I'd be home soon. This was the first they had heard that I was still alive and finally free, and they were almost hysterical with laughing and crying. Then I called Jane P————-, up in Westover, Mass. She made me promise to come to see her, and I did. In another day, my travel orders were cut to Fort Sam Houston in San Antonio, and after happy but sad farewells to Kohlrabi John Frawley and Bob Sage, I boarded the bus to San Antonio.

At Fort Sam, I was processed again, examined again—I was clearly gaining weight fast—had a pot belly, I think—and issued new underwear, socks, shoes, and two Class A khaki uniforms plus a $500 advance against back pay, (I think it was the most money at one time that I had ever had in my life), and a 60-day R&R [rest and relaxation] furlough.

I went to the PX and bought Tech Sgt. stripes (three chevrons with two rockers), wings, and ribbons for the decorations that I knew for sure I had, and the 15th Air Force insignia shoulder patch, all of which I proudly affixed to my brand new uniforms. Carefully packing all my Brit issue in my new barracks bag, I again boarded the bus for the last leg of my voyage home.

I don't remember for sure, but I seem to recall that I arrived in Lubbock on May 16, 1945, exactly one month after our liberation date!

I had not called home since Fort Dix. I wanted to surprise the folks, so I took a cab from the bus station out to the house on 29th Street.

I walked up to the front door which was open, and hollered, "Anybody home?!" Mother was in the kitchen and came running and screaming to the front door, and I held the screen door shut against her for a minute until she almost tore it down.

Needless to say, it was a joyful reunion. Dad was home too and they called Sug at nursing school downtown and pretty soon she arrived. I related some of the highlights (or lowlights) of some of the adventures I have chronicled here, and learned the sad news that my best buddy through basic training, radio and gunnery schools, and crew training, Mel King from Akron, Ohio, had been shot down and killed on his first mission over Germany with the 8th Air Force. Mrs. King had my home address from Mel and had written Mother to tell her and to ask about me.

Mother had also heard from Ted Poole's wife in Houston and I had the sad duty later of writing a long letter to her telling her the details of Ted's last mission.

But it was more gladness than sadness and 60 whole beautiful glorious days of freedom stretched in front of me.

More later.

Love,
Skip

Chapter 17
Back at Home
"It was not like it had been before. I now had the elemental knowledge of the experiences of life and death."

Manzanillo, Colima, Mexico
____ de Mayo 1989 [inadvertently undated]

Dear Cindy Lou,

When you asked me to write about my experience as a POW, I felt that I had to give you some background to put you in the context of the time and places and circumstances that then existed in order to give you a better perspective. When this started out I had no intention of writing an autobiography of the whole war from my *own* perspective, but it grew into that and I might as well finish it. We are almost there!

I don't remember many details of my R&R leave. In my last report I think I said it was 60 days, but casting my mind's eye back on the chronology of events during that time, it could have been at the most about 45 days, or even 30 days. Your dad was at Roswell AFB in New Mexico—I don't remember what he was doing there—it doesn't matter—but since he couldn't come home, I went over to Roswell and spent several days with him, helling around town and getting drunk with him and his buddies. After that I came back to Lubbock, then I took a train for the long trip to Springfield, Mass (near Westover), and spent several days with Jane, her mother and younger sister. Their older brother was still in the service in the Pacific.

This visit, though wonderful at the time, was inconclusive at the end as far as Jane and I were concerned. We were still both very young—she was Catholic (strongly) and I was Protestant—we lived a terribly long way apart and I was still in the service for the duration and the war in the Pacific was still going strong. So we parted on a tentative basis with nothing settled between us.

On the return trip, I had routed myself back through Buffalo, NY and was met at the depot by your mother, Beth, whom I had never met, but of course had heard a lot about, and I had seen pictures of her. As you probably know, she and your dad met at the graduation and commissioning exercises at Enid, Oklahoma, when your dad and his buddy Arnold (I think that was his name), Beth's cousin, graduated from cadet school. They later became engaged, and I had written Beth from Lubbock about my trip to Mass. and she had written back inviting me to stop over a few days in Grand Island. We had an absolutely marvelous time. Beth and your Grandma Elsie were wonderful hostesses and I met all the family and all the friends on Grand Island. Beth took me to Niagara Falls and I think people there must have thought we were honeymooners! We went across the bridge to Hamilton (is it?), Canada, and did everything there was to do! Next time you see your Mom, ask her if she remembers when I visited her and Elsie in Grand Island!

Then back to Lubbock and I don't remember much more of that leave. I had no girlfriend in Lubbock and most of my old friends from Tech were either dead or still in the service. So when I received orders through the mail from the Air Corps to report to a certain hotel in Miami Beach, Florida, I was ready to go. The Armed Services had taken over almost all the hotels on Miami Beach for R&R and administrative purposes. After checking into the hotel, meeting up with some other ex-kriegies I knew (one of them was Bill Louder from Lubbock), we spent time on the beach, raised what hell we could in town, and enjoyed ourselves for a couple of days.

Then we went through a series of intense grilling from officers and men of the OSS (forerunner to the CIA) about the details of our capture, our interrogation by the Germans, and almost every day, day by day, details of our life in the German POW camps. They were a little amused at my account of mine, Sage's and Kohlrabi John's "escape" at Fallingboestal, but I assured them that at the time, it was not so goddamn funny!

After the OSS finished with us, we were interviewed by regular Air Corps people, giving us the options as to what duty we could apply for the duration of the war. We were in for the "duration" unless eligible for discharge for physical disability and the fact that we had been POWs did not count, unless it contributed enough to the "disability." I did not feel "disabled." In fact, I felt fine, full of piss and vinegar. I had regained all my lost weight and was in fact probably a little overweight. So I was not looking for a discharge out of pity and sympathy. After all the options were spelled out, I signed up for crew training on the B-29 SuperForts and duty in the Pacific.

I did not want to be an instructor in either radio or gunnery school, and the other options (I don't remember what they were) had no attraction for me at all. So, I was assigned back to dear old Scott Field, Illinois, for a refresher course in radio and specific training on the B-29 radio systems! I was elated to be going back to Scott.

My memory of the chronology of these last events is very hazy, but I think I arrived at Scott in early July 1945. The old saying is true—"you can't go home again." Scott Field had changed. St. Louis had changed and I had changed. None of my old buddies were there. Scott Field administration seemed to be in some disarray. There was a sudden large influx of people like myself from the European theater who were awaiting retraining for assignments in the Pacific.

They still had their recruits from basic training who were going through what us old-timers had been through before. And us old-timers were not raw recruits out of basic training, we were veteran non-coms, staff and tech sargeants. And they did not have these new "refresher" courses yet set up, nor the classes for training on the B-29 radio systems. So there was a lot of confusion and backing and filling. They ended up giving us "permanent" passes. We did not meet roll calls, we had no duties, we could come and go as we pleased. We could go into St. Louis (or wherever) whenever we wanted. It sounded like Heaven in military life, but it was boring. I went into St. Louis a lot, and went to the Browns and Cardinals baseball games, USO dances, etc. and went back to the old jazz honkytonks in East St. Louis—but it was not like it had been before. I now had the elemental knowledge of the experience of life and death, and I shied away from relating to anybody very closely, and had no real friends. There were many like me.

The war in the Pacific dragged on and the Japanese resistance was fanatical; more even than the Germans had been. The Air Corps B-29s kept up a continual bombardment of all the Japanese-held Pacific Islands and the U.S. Marines and Infantry took each one at great loss of lives. There was a tremendous buildup of all Allied Forces in the Pacific for the final invasion of the Japanese Islands themselves. The B-29s were bombing the home islands against the same kamikaze fighters that were attacking the Allied fleet ships. I listened to the radio and read the newspapers, and said to myself "you silly son-of-a-bitch, why did you sign up for this, when you could have...." I had no answer except that I had signed up for the "duration" and that the goddamned war was still "enduring!"

Then in early August came the awesome news of the bomb dropped on Hiroshima, and a few days later on Nagasaki, and a few days later [August 14, 1945] Japan's unconditional surrender. I cannot begin to describe to you the awful, terrible impact that that news unleashed upon the world. First of course there was the unthinking joy among the Allied world that victory had been achieved and that the long bloody war on both sides of the earth was at last at an end. It was only later that the consequences of what we had done in splitting and harnessing the power of the atom became apparent. We had ushered in a new era in world history. You were born in this era and have known nothing else so it is difficult for your generation to realize the impact those events had on those who were born and lived in the previous era.

Like everyone else, I was overjoyed that the war was over and that the dreaded invasion of Japan's home islands was not necessary and that I now did not have to go to the Pacific Theater. But oddly, after the first several days I fell into sort of a blue funk. I simply didn't know what to do! We had all looked forward hopefully to the war's end, but I (like many others I'm sure) had never given any real thought to life beyond that. I guess I just had always assumed that I would pick up where I left off and go on from there. But life had changed—I had changed—things were more complicated now. There were more things to be considered, more options available, and choices to be made. This had come suddenly and I simply wasn't ready to consider those options and make those choices. So I drifted—mindlessly going through the now meaningless military routine asking myself, "What do I do now?"

I thought of staying in the service. I could easily have qualified for Officer Candidate School. I thought about applying for cadet school to become a pilot, but now with no need for thousands of fighters and bombers in the air, the Air Corps found itself with an embarrassing surplus of airplane drivers. I thought of staying in as an enlisted man—I was a high ranking NCO, but I couldn't think of what I would *do*. Somehow the idea of going back to Texas Tech and journalism school now seemed puerile. I was more drawn toward electronics and communications, but it would mean almost starting over from scratch at school and almost three years were already gone.

So the August days drifted into September and early October.

The Air Corps had set up a point system for its demobilization program—so many points for length of service, so many points for foreign duty, for medals, honors, decorations won, etc. (Oddly enough, there were no points for POW time except it counted as "foreign duty!") One day in early October, I wandered over to the Separation Center out of curiosity to find out how many points I had. Somewhat to my surprise, I found I had more than enough to apply for immediate discharge.

Within the week I had made up my mind—electronics and communications. So I received my discharge on October 14, 1945, and hitchhiked home from St. Louis to Lubbock just for the fun of it! It was easy then. Anybody would pick up a service man.

I got home, wrote to every engineering school in the country for catalogs and admission applications and applied at Tech for readmission in the January '46 term as a math major. Tech had a good electrical engineering school but it was all power—no electronics or communications. I knew I would need more math than I had to be accepted in any engineering school, so when I went back to re-enroll at Tech, I signed up for all the math courses I could. I was required to take two social studies courses, so I signed up for first year Spanish and because I had always been curious about it, Psychology 101A.

In the first psychology class in mid-January well before the bell had rung, a tall, slender, pretty girl with long brown hair and a slight gap between her two front teeth came in late. She was rather breathless and took a vacant seat, one over from me. I kept looking at her and thinking, *Hmm, I think I might like to get to know her.*

Her name was Nikki Whaley.

And so, one story was ended and another had begun!

Your lovin' Uncle,
Skip

[My uncle did marry the "tall, slender, pretty girl"—my Aunt Nikki. But his new story was not to be written.]

Chapter 18
Message to His Children
"If there was ever a 'just' war, this one seemed to be it."

Manzanillo, Colima, Mexico
Sat., May 27, 1989

[Handwritten at the top of this photocopy of Weldon's letter to his children]:
Cindy—thought I should send you a copy of this, to sort of complete your "records."

Love,
Skip

To all my children,

   Wasn't that once the title of a long-running soap opera? Well, I am soon to unveil to you, or perhaps impose upon you, several scenes and segments of something of a soap opera, autobiographical, that concerned my life from around 1939, the beginning of World War II, until early 1946, the ending of WWII and its immediate aftermath. This has to do of course with my experiences in the service and as a prisoner of war in Germany. Some of these experiences and some specific incidents I have related to some of you, orally, when asked. I don't think I had ever had any reticence about discussing those events with you whenever you exhibited an interest in them. But I had never volunteered a compete detailed description of those events partly because I thought it would seem like ancient history to you, partly because I was not asked and I presume this to be a complicated mixture of some disinterest—and some reluctance on your parts—to have the old man relive a painful past; and partly because over the years, I had actually forgotten many of the details of those far-gone-in-time happenings.

In January 1988 in Lubbock at Sug's funeral, I was reunited after too many years with one of my favorite people, your cousin Cindy. After I came to Mexico in early May 1988, Cindy and I developed a correspondence based at first on our mutual interest in Mexican history, geography, flora and fauna, which later developed into more personal, family affairs. During the course of this correspondence, Cindy asked me in one letter if I would tell her of my experiences as a POW in Germany. I of course agreed to do so.

But when I attempted to do this, I found I could not separate those experiences from the wider context of the war in which they occurred, and the historical circumstances of that time. So, in order to give her a broader perspective of those events, I wound up giving her the whole history of the war from my own perspective, starting from before U.S. participation in that war in December 1941. Somewhere during the recitation of those events, I realized that what I was doing had relevance to all of you, and I asked Cindy to make copies of all my letters and send to Lee for re-copying and distribution to all of you.

Before you read that story, I feel as I did with Cindy, that I must put that story itself within its own broader historical perspective for you. Maybe that will give you a better understanding of the times, and perhaps even of your old man!

As you know, I was brought up in the countryside and small towns of West Texas during the depression with a rather strict upbringing bearing heavily on ethics and morality and hard work. In school, we were taught American and Texas history with a strong, patriotic bias. The negative sides of both histories were ignored or glossed over. I could never decide if I were prouder to be an American or a Texan— I guess I was equally proud of being both. It never occurred to me that my country could ever be, or do, wrong, or that its affairs were run by men of greater or lesser aptitudes. To me, being President of the United States conferred the greatness of Washington, of Jefferson, of Lincoln, or of Roosevelt, upon the incumbent. So I, like most of my generation, grew up with a strong, unquestioning patriotism.

As events unfolded in Europe in the mid to late '30s, they only served to strengthen those feelings. It is easy to see in retrospect that the war could have been avoided, or at least sharply restricted, if the democracies of Europe had called Hitler's bluffs earlier when he was really bluffing. The U.S. too could have and should have played a stronger hand against Hitler. But all governments are run by fallible people and they dawdled, played politics, fawned and cringed until the horrible war came to be inevitable, along with our own eventual involvement in it. But if there was ever a "just" war, this one seemed to be it, and all America was fired up to fight it.

For several years after the war, I maintained the same uncritical attitude. Times were good, Europe was recovering with help from the U.S. under the Marshall Plan, and the "Reds" had become the new enemy, the new Satan. But a number of things had begun to bother me. I had learned—*long* after it had happened—of the forced internment of American citizens—not by some foreign power—but by the American government itself, simply because of their Japanese ancestry. They had committed no crime, they had not been charged, they had not been tried, yet they were imprisoned by their fellow citizens from early 1942 until the end of the war in 1945. This had been done with a great deal of secrecy as far as the American public was concerned—if there were news accounts of it, they were buried by the "larger" news of the war and this was as the Government wanted it. This action was even condoned and sanctioned and declared to be "constitutional" by the U.S. Supreme Court!! These people were never compensated for the loss of their properties, their businesses, their jobs or salaries! [Years later after he wrote this letter, some Japanese-Americans were reimbursed for their interment. The Japanese-American Internment Memorial was unveiled in San Jose, California on March 5, 1994.] This bothered me greatly after I learned of it, years later. It seemed to me to be a most heinous act that could have only been perpetuated in Nazi Germany!

Even earlier, the "Red-baiting" and the witch hunts in both houses of Congress led me to begin to question the purity of the motives of the men who led our government. In the Senate, Joe McCarthy ("Tail-Gunner Joe"—he had been in the 8th Air Force) got away with ruining the lives, careers and reputations of many people, by smears and innuendoes. He was finally stopped, and toppled from power by the courage of a radio/TV newsman, Edward Murrow, and only belatedly censured by his colleagues in the Senate after it was politically safe to do so. In the House, the "House Un-American Activities Committee" did a similar job on innocent people in the entertainment world, creating guilt by association—the infamous Hollywood Black List—and through intimidation and threats of imprisonment for "contempt of Congress," forced people to testify against friends and colleagues who had been communists. During the war when Russia had been our "staunch ally," it had become fashionable for so-called intellectuals and people in entertainment to join the Communist Party. Most of them dropped out in disillusionment after a short while, but they had tainted themselves for life; in this Post-War era of "Red" hysteria and paranoia, their "patriotism" was called into question by contemptible men. It was difficult not to feel contempt for that Congress!

And even earlier than *that*, I had been appalled at the way our government let some of our citizens be treated. In early 1948, your Mom and I (and Lee) were in New York City, where I was going to school, and looking for an apartment. I was touched and amazed at what a good, Christian city New York was. Nearly all the ads closed at the bottom with the line "Christians only need apply." I was even more amazed at my own naivete and stupidity when I later learned that that meant "Jews don't bother!" But how could people do that to other people—a people who had just recently barely escaped total genocide in Europe!! And how could our government permit it?! Of course it did not occur to me at that time to recognize and realize that we had for years been doing far worse to Blacks!

But I still had some illusions left and still had faith and trust in our government to do the "right thing." I remember when we were living in Dallas, in 1963 I think it was, and [President] Kennedy was slowly but surely getting us more and more involved in Viet Nam [at that time, Vietnam was popularly spelled as two separate words], sending over more military "advisors." Lee and I got into a somewhat heated argument over our policy toward Viet Nam, about our motives for being there, and what goals we wanted to accomplish. In the heat of the argument, I even had the temerity to question his patriotism. I hope he has forgotten that, but I remembered it with shame every day he was in Viet Nam years later, and still do. I feared for his life every day that he was over there, and hated LBJ [Lyndon Baines Johnson who became president following Kennedy's assassination and who further escalated the Vietnam War] for the chicanery with which he had maneuvered us ever deeper into that war. Our reasons and purposes for being there were too nebulous, too dim, too undefined, to put the life of my son, and thousands of others at risk!

By the time the tawdry Nixon/Agnew affairs came to light [the "Watergate" scandal, stemming from a break-in at the offices of the Democratic National Committee during the 1972 presidential campaign, causing President Nixon to resign in 1974], I had no illusions left, but I was still aghast at the pettiness and in Agnew's case [Vice President Spiro Agnew resigned in 1973 after being fined for income tax evasion], simple thievery and greed, of the two men who had been honored with the highest two offices in our land. I was not surprised at the bumbling, two-dimensional Reagan and his bully boys in the CIA and the NSA [National Security Agency], when the Iran/Contra scandal broke. How Reagan managed to bamboozle the American public for 8 years, and maintain his image as a "Great Communicator," I will never understand. His single-minded, blind obsession with Nicaragua was paranoid, and his likening of the Contra rebels to "our founding fathers" was blasphemy! They were (and are) for the most part, holdovers from the National Guards that served the two previous Somoza regimes, that held Nicaragua under cruel tyranny for decades while our government supported them and other dictators around the world.

Let me hasten to assure you that my disillusionment has been with men, with people. The office of the Presidency does not automatically bestow greatness and statesmanship upon an incumbent. Only rarely does a Washington, a Jefferson, or a Lincoln come along. But I do have faith and trust in our form and system of government, and in that noble document, the Constitution, which has withstood the ravages of Nixon/Agnew and Reagan, and even a savage civil war. The great ideals of liberty, freedom, and justice inherent in that document are what we strive to live by, and what keeps this country great. However unwise our policies may be, foreign or domestic, however ineptly and foolishly they may be formulated and carried out by bumbling leaders, I still think that by and large those leaders and the people are still guided by the Constitution and those great ideals that document engenders.

So I am still a "patriot," albeit a somewhat cynical one. One of our wise forefathers once said "the price of liberty is eternal vigilance" [Thomas Jefferson (1743-1826)] and he was right! We must exercise more care in choosing our leaders, from the local level on up, and then watch what they do, and call their account. I am saddened to see the ever decreasing turnout of the electorate and the seeming indifference of the masses of people to their governmental processes and their participation. If we are not careful—if we don't participate, if we do not exercise that "eternal vigilance"—someday, God forbid, we may elect a Hitler.

I hope the war stories enlighten you and maybe answer some questions you may have had—and never asked. I will be interested to hear any comments you may wish to make, or answer any further questions you may have.

God bless and keep you all.

Your loving Dad

Chapter 19
The End Nears
"About the war stories, Hon...I am through and finished..."

Houston, Texas
June 10, 1989

Querida Tio Mio,

In pulling up my computer files, I see it was April when I last wrote you. The last time I was even at my computer was when I was working on my draft for the article for *Aviation Week*. I spent two and a half days at my old green monochrome terminal doing a 27-page draft and after that, I couldn't bear to even look at my computer! I do a lot of work like that at home where it is more quiet with son Ben in school than at the office where I am constantly interrupted. The article for *Aviation Week* is the biggest writing project I have done. When it comes out in the July 17th issue, I will send you one. At work, I have three different word processors that I work on—all of them different from each other and the one I have at home. I find when I work on one machine, I have to stop and learn it all over again, it seems.

I am sending you a copy of the letters you have sent me. I thought it might be better for you to include or make additional notes if you want. Anyway, send what you want to Lee. I am pleased that I could be a part of this. I think anyone who reads what you have written cannot help but be moved and have new understanding of that time and the overall impact of WWII on everyone's lives. Please let me know what else I can do and how I can assist in distributing your story.

I am also sending you information about the POW medal. The number I called had a recording that said POWs of WWI, WWII, Korea and Vietnam were eligible, but missing-in-action and hostages were not. (Interesting.) Said to leave your name and address on the recording and an application would be sent to you. Complete as best as possible, then mail to appropriate branch of service. The application and return envelope came to me in yesterday's mail and I am forwarding them on to you. I hope you will complete it and send it in. Again, please let me know if I can assist on this in any way. I have made copies of the form for my information. Should you need an extra, let me know. I was sorry to hear that your other medals were lost in the 1970 tornado in Lubbock. Maybe you should get them replaced.

I am returning your pictures. Nice fish! I am getting the hankering to go to Mexico. I have been working full-time at my part-time job for over a month now on this *Aviation Week* project. Just last Friday, I sent the photos and illustrations to the publisher in New York to be included in the article. Forgive me for going on about this, but this project has taken up the bulk of my life for the past few months. There is still long-distance editing to do by phone and fax until the second week of July. It really has been exciting and there is a chance I may be writing more articles like this.

I talked to Mom on the phone yesterday and asked her if she remembered when you came to visit her in New York. She did, and has many happy memories of it. She said to ask you if you remember her cousin Art telling you that you were the lucky one and you answered, "No, she is marrying my brother." Cousin Art answered, "I know. That's why you're the lucky one!" Mom said when she and Dad were later stationed in Germany, they took some home movies and you were able to recognize some areas and pick out some points of interest in Germany and Austria.

When I read that you were freed by General Monty, I vowed to never to call him a fuzzy britches again as I am prone to do when I watch the movie *Patton*. I love that movie and don't know how many times I have seen it. I had always thought you were liberated by the

Russian army. I think Dad told me that or I might be mistaken.

You asked about some books of Robert A. Heinlein. Probably his most commercially popular (but not my favorite) was *Stranger in a Strange Land* that came out circa 1961. It became a "cult classic." In this book, Heinlien termed the work "grok" and all the modern dictionaries now include grok ("to understand thoroughly because of having empathy with"). I am sending you *Farnham's Freehold* to see if you like it. Please return it to me. It is Becky's book. She and I are trying to get a collection together of all his writings.

If it seems my subject matter is jumping around, it is because I am going through some of your last letters and commenting. I remember Dad telling us about General Taylor and his wife. If I remember right, she was pregnant at the time she jumped out of the plane. I've written Dad and asked him to tell me about his experiences, but so far I haven't received a reply. [Dad never did talk about it, but years later Mother gave me all the newspaper clippings of the event that she had saved.]

I don't know about the family reunion yet. I have it on the calendar and we'll have to see as we get closer to it. But by all means, please plan on staying with us as long as you like. We would love to see you and get to visit with you and show you the area. We absolutely love Houston—at least the area where we live. Right behind the space center. Which reminds me. I like your phrasing of "Dr. von Braun and his Black Forest elves." Von Braun, as you know, was one of the German rocket scientists that our country was able to grab at the fall of Peenemunde. The Russians grabbed the others and that's what started the space race. Von Braun was in Mission Control here at the time of Apollo 11 in July 1969. I think the story of the rush to grab German rocket scientists at Peenemunde was best told in James Michener's book, *Space*.

Speaking of books, you mentioned *Catch 22*. You will be happy to know that it was required reading when I was in high school. I like C.S. Lewis too, though I haven't read much of him. He was a professor who started out studying the Bible to debunk it intellectually, then ended up being a staunch believer.

Ben received your card and the t-shirt on the very day of his graduation! You will be hearing from him shortly. He went through the graduation ceremony, but lacks half a credit to complete high school, so he will be attending three weeks of summer school this summer. He told us yesterday he plans to get an apartment with a friend the end of this month when he has finished summer school. I hope that idea dies on the vine before then.

I am also enjoying the beautiful Mexican postage stamps that you are using. I don't collect stamps, but I am keeping the ones you are sending.

I guess this is all the news for now. I hope this package reaches you safely; if not, I have copies. I really hope to see you in Houston later this summer if not earlier in Mexico! We really do like Mexico. I have not been to Cozumel and would like to see that fair island.

Hope this finds you happy and well. Please continue to write.

Love,
Cindy

Manzanillo, Colima Mexico
27 de Junio 1989

Dear Cindy Lou,

I received your package surprisingly quickly, and thank you very much for the very good copies—that must have been a lot of work. I just read through it quickly and forwarded it to Lee without changes or additions. Now that it is over and done with, I'm through with it—it's all yours and Lee's. I only sent him the part pertaining to the war.

Thanks also for enclosing the Heinlein book—I have already read it and thoroughly enjoyed it—I could easily become a sci-fi buff. Unfortunately I am a fast reader and I find I go through my reading material all too quickly. If it's OK with you I will bring the book with me when I come to Texas—I don't trust the mails with anything valuable.

I am looking forward to reading your article in *Aviation Week*. When I worked at Ampex I used to read that mag regularly. Both the Air Force and NASA were (and I suppose still are) good Ampex customers for instrumentation and video recording equipment. When I was still with the domestic division way back, I used to call occasionally at the old Redstone Arsenal in Huntsville [Alabama, where NASA's Marshall Spaceflight Center is also located]. I also called fairly often at White Sands [New Mexico, where NASA and the Army have rocket/missile facilities]—we had a lot of equipment there, and several on-site contract engineers. This was when I was working out of the Atlanta office, and later, Dallas, before we moved to California.

I was amused at your remarks about Monty. He and Patton were direct opposites, and both together gave poor old Ike almost as much trouble as the Germans.

I had forgotten about the repartee with your mother's cousin Art, about who the "lucky one" was but I remembered it when you mentioned it. I'm glad Beth remembers so much of that occasion—those were happier days, even with the war.

Not much news from here—the rains have come finally, a month and a half later than normal. We have had two big storms, with heavy rain, high winds, and lots of thunder and lightning. On the second one, there was a small hurricane centered off the coast of Acupulco, considerably south and east of here, and we were in the northwest edge of it, and really got pelted. For several days the surf was higher than I have ever seen it—the waves rolling in twelve to fifteen feet high before cresting over and throwing heavy white foam 30 feet into the air. Spectacular! The water came right up to the sea wall.

I'm really looking forward to seeing you, either here, the reunion, or Houston, whichever comes first. In the meantime please stay in touch.

Con much cariño,
Tio Skip

Houston, Texas
July 20, 1989

Dear Uncle Skip,

Today is the 20th anniversary of the Apollo 11 lunar landing. It has been receiving wide coverage from here locally on the national networks. In fact, President Bush is to announce a new direction for the country's space program here today. Tonight, the three Apollo 11 astronauts will be in town to celebrate the exact moment when Neil Armstrong first set foot on the moon (9:56 p.m. Houston time). There will be boats on the water displaying all their lights and a laser show over the lake. This afternoon, there will be several fly-overs by military jets. It's been an exciting week so far.

I am enclosing a copy of the market supplement that was included in Monday's issue of *Aviation Week*. My boss tells me that we may be doing one on space. I think that would be great. For the past two weeks, my schedule has slacked off and I am on part-time hours at work. I will stay part-time through the end of this year because I am taking additional writing classes this fall. Then, after school is out in mid-December and after the holidays, I will work full-time on the National Space Trophy project again. What I do is the press releases, the program for the ceremony in February, and a press conference with the featured speaker and honoree. Last year, the recipient of the National Space Trophy was Rear Adm. Richard Truly, now the head administrator of NASA. This year we are hoping to have Vice President Quayle as the featured speaker. President Bush was already committed to something else in February.

I'm glad the copies of your narrative came out all right and you received them in good shape. Mother told me that she would be interested in reading your account, and I said I would ask you first.

Glad, too, that you liked the Heinlein book. Yes, of course you can return it when we see you. I would send you another now, but I don't have any more tear-resistant plastic envelopes that are good for those kind of mailings.

I don't think we are going to make it to the reunion this year. I wanted to let you know that we will be in Cozumel August 25-28 with an insurance convention. I know that doesn't sound very exciting, but they are good friends of ours. We may find ourselves back in the aviation insurance business some day. Anyway, we are staying at the Plaza las Glorias in Cozumel and would love to see you there. Let me know if you think you can make it. I plan to do some snorkeling and see the tank with the "tame" sharks. (This I gotta see. Sounds like a tourist gimmick to me. As I understand it, you can get in the tank with these sharks and have your picture taken with them. That would make a nice photo to put over the mantle! Especially if I was wearing a t-shirt that says "Macho, schmacho. Hemingway was a wimp!")

Speaking of Hemingway, they just found a diary of his and a "Dear John" letter that he received from his first love when he was 19. She was seven years older than he. When she called off their romance in the letter, she called him a "boy" and then as a *coup de grace*, told him she was marrying someone else. This has led to further speculation about his feelings toward women and his machismo.

I hope you received a thank you note from Ben. He successfully finished summer school and received his diploma. He moved out about three weeks ago to an apartment close by. I really don't mind, but can't help but worry about him. But I understand how he wants to be independent. We talk several times a week. He tells me he is having to adjust to living with someone after being an only child. And that he doesn't like too many people around and too much excitement going on. We have a pretty quiet home life. He asked me to go see the movie *Batman* with him the other night. Batman is the latest rage in the country now (again). In fact the Air Force just revealed the new Stealth Bomber and the press called it the "Batwing" because that's what it looks like. Do you get an American newspaper there?

A tropical storm hit the Texas coast and we had all sorts of rain, but no flooding in our immediate area. We had so much rain that by the time it cleared up and I was able to clean out my bird feeder. It had 6-inch sprouts from the bird seed. Now the weather is mostly hot and humid.

We are really looking forward to your stay with us. Please plan to spend some time here. There is so much to do and see. Plus after so many years, it will be nice to spend some time with you.

Hope this finds you happy and well. Hope to see you in Cozumel.

Love,
Cindy

Manzanillo, Colima, Mexico
1 de Agosto 1989

Received your letter and *Aviation Week* article yesterday. You should be very proud of yourself, it is an excellent piece of work and very professional! I am proud of you! I also thought the cover montage was great. Do you know the artist/photographer?

Your articles brought back vivid memories of those days. I had forgotten exactly *when* it was, but I'll never forget the compelling drama of those events, as we all sat glued in front of the TV set. Later that night I went out in the front yard and looked up at the full moon with my binoculars. A foolish gesture perhaps, but it did seem to bring it closer. Like you, I too would give my eyeteeth to go into space. When you see Adm. Truly again, tell him your have an old unk you need to have along to carry your briefcase. I could bring my Nikon F-3 and take some pix to go with your articles!

Sounds like you have a busy time ahead with school, and then the Space Trophy. Like Mother, I hope you win it!

Dear Heart, your trips to Mexico and mine to the states always seem to conflict. I would love to join you all in Cozumel, but I am leaving here on August 26 heading for Lubbock. I am going by train this time, to get to see more of the country. Will go from here to Guadalajara, thence to Cuidad de Mexico, thence to Nuevo Laredo via Monterrey. First class fare including two nights and a Pullman compartment is $68.00! I will fly from Laredo to Lubbock. The reunion is September 3, and I will call you sometime after that—and maybe we can set something up to get together a bit—but I certainly don't want to disrupt your busy schedule.

I did receive a very nice thank you note from Ben, more than the stereotypical thank you note—he told me a little about his plans and his job, and asked me some questions about Mexico. He sounds like a very nice kid, and I would like to get to know him. Mother told me that Kurtis [my brother Jerry's son] received some fabulous scholarship from the University of Texas, but she didn't tell me any details. I feel ashamed of myself, I used to keep in fairly close touch with Jerry and his wife, but I haven't written or called them since I have been down here. I will call them when I get to Lubbock.

About the war stories, Hon, by all means send them (or copies) to Beth, and anyone else (your Dad) whom you think may have any interest in wading through them. I am through and finished with it, and glad it is over, and it is all yours and Lee's. I suppose it did have some cathartic effect, even after all these years (45 years ago day after tomorrow I was shot down), and I did rather vividly re-live some of those events as I was recalling them. But anyway, the thing is yours to do with as you please, Dear Heart.

It's been a long, hot humid summer! Rain, rain, rain, all night last night, and all day today. But at least there's been cloud cover all day, and a slight breeze and it has been pleasantly cool. Early in the season (rainy season) there was a hurricane off the coast of Acupulco, considerably southeast of here. I think that may have been the same storm you mentioned hitting the Texas coast. We were in the northwest edge of it and had gale winds, torrential rains and spectacular lightning and thunder. For several days afterwards the surf was higher than I had ever seen it.

Like most sea level cities, the drainage is poor, and the present rains have made rivers of the streets and miniature lakes of all open, level spots. Luckily, I have a mini-super about 200 meters up the street where I am able to wade to replenish my supply of beer!

Mucho cariño from
your lovin' Unk

[Weldon did come to visit in Houston. He wrote about it to my grandparents, then sent me a copy of his letter to them.]

Manzanillo, Colima, Mexico
21 Sept. 1989

Dear Cindy Lou,

Why write two letters when one will do? I was going to write you
a thank you letter after I had written the folks, then decided I would
just send you a copy of that—to let you know how much I enjoyed my
visit!

Y'all come, y'hear!

Love,
Skip

[Photocopy of letter:]

Dear Mother and Dad,

I really enjoyed my stay at home, the reunion, eating too much,
doing my shopping, and doing what I could around the house, and
visiting with B. Tell Buddy and Kitty I'm sorry I missed seeing them,
and I wish I could have seen Connie more, but I realize how busy she
is. I also enjoyed the cool weather—it will be awhile before I have
that again!

Also had a great time in Houston. Cindy met my plane (on time—
actually a few minutes early), and we drove out to her townhouse
southeast of Houston near Clear Lake and NASA's Johnson Space
Center. Cindy and I sat up and visited for awhile, then turned in. Next
day, Cindy had the day off (or at least so she said) and we spent a nice
lazy day finishing up my shopping (puzzle books, gift candy, etc.),
and booking my flight out Sunday through a travel agent Cindy
knows. We drove all around the Clear Lake area, with Cindy pointing
out all the sights and we had a nice lunch of fried shrimp and oysters
and beer at a little lakeside joint. Clear Lake is salt water, it is joined
by a channel to Galveston Bay, and it is ringed almost all the way

around with boat marinas and seafood places.

Friday morning I lazed around the house, read the paper and watched TV. She has cable, so there was lots to see. Cindy had classes—she's taking creative writing courses at a nearby college, and works part-time at an advertising agency whose major clients are aerospace companies, so Cindy does a lot of writing and PR [public relations] work for the space program, and is well up on everything that goes on in space. Some of her projects have been keeping her busy more than full-time. She came home at noon and fixed lunch, hoping to have the afternoon off, but she had to go to work, so she dropped me off over at the Johnson Space Center where I spent the whole afternoon poking into every nook and cranny where they let feather merchants go. It's a fabulous place, like a huge college campus, beautifully kept, and with museum-type exhibits of all the artifacts representing the entire history of the space age. I saw moon rocks, and the actual Mercury and Gemini capsules the early astronauts flew in, and the Apollo craft that went to the moon and returned—and a model of the Skylab that was in space for so long— it was *huge*! And the space shuttle mockup that the present day astronauts use for training. All in all it was a truly fascinating day for me!

Cindy picked me up a little after 5, and that evening took me out to dinner at a restaurant at a marina. I had a filet-mignon, about an inch and a half thick, but so tender and juicy it almost melted in your mouth—ooh, it was delicious! I haven't had such a good steak in I don't know when!

Next morning (Saturday) Cindy and I had a lazy breakfast of scrambled eggs and the remains of the filet-mignon which I couldn't finish the night before. Later on we went crabbing (for blue crabs) down by the lakeside. This is a highly sophisticated form of fishing requiring a lot of expensive equipment and extensive knowledge of marine life! What you do is tie a long piece of string around a raw chicken neck, throw it into the water, and when you feel a crab gently tugging on it, you inch your line in very slowly until you can get a dipnet under it, and haul that sucker in! I caught two—both too small to keep—and poor Cindy didn't catch a one, which proves how good a natural fisherman I am—she with all the experience and me with none at crabbing!

Well, this was hard, tiring and thirsty work, which prompted a visit to a nearby Cajun joint for a cold beer. We hadn't intended to eat lunch, but the waitress cannily left two menus at the table, and soon we had crawfish *ettoufee*, Cajun beans and rice, barbecued froglegs wrapped in bacon strips, barbecued shrimp and barbecued blue crab! Wow! Hadn't had such food since I was last in Breau Bridge, Louisiana, at the crawdad festival!

Later that evening, we met her friends at a boat where we weighed anchor and set out through the channel into Galveston Bay. It was a *beautiful* evening—the front that went through Lubbock had reached Houston by the time I got there—it had brought a little rain, but mostly clear weather with balmy sunshine and cool breezes and a little fall snap to the air that was absolutely delightful. The "boat" was a 35-foot Bertram cabin cruiser with twin Chrysler 415 hp engines that can push that baby up to 35 knots! I love sailboats and have always considered myself a "sailor," but when I get on a power cruiser like that one, I can easily be converted! It was a beautiful cruise—we came back into Clear Lake and anchored awhile off the Hilton Hotel and its marina and watched a gorgeous full moon rise over the water.

Sunday morning Cindy takes me to the airport for a 10:35 a.m. flight. I am on Continental direct to Ixtapa, a small resort town south of here, then change to Mexicana for a 50-minute flight back up the coast to Manzanillo. Arrive home about 3:30 p.m. (4:30 p.m. your time) and all is well.

It has been raining steadily ever since my return, night and day. The seas are up—not as high as I wrote you earlier, but still pretty spectacular. The steady rain makes it difficult to get around without getting wet, but at least it keeps the temperature down—it's really quite pleasant. The hot water heater is out of commish—don't know what the problem is—I used the last of the hot water Monday morn to take a tepid shower. Since then I have been heating four tea kettles

(8 liters) of water every morning, pouring it in a large pail, stand in the shower, pour a little over me, soap up, then use the rest to rinse off good. Not too bad—reminds me of how we used to shower in a POW barracks! And at least it is not cold here! Oh, well, this is Mexico—and the water heater will be fixed sooner or later!

Went up to Santiago Monday night and watched the first half of the Denver/Buffalo game at my hamburger joint. I was too tired and sleepy to stay for the second half. That blue crab fishing really takes it out of you!

Write soon.

Con much cariño,
Weldon

P.S. Had sealed and addressed this and started a "bread and butter" thank you note to Cindy about my visit, when I realized that this letter could better convey to her how much I enjoyed my Houston visit than I ever could directly express. So I made a copy of it to send to her.

Skip

EPILOGUE

I never did travel back to Santiago, Mexico, to see my uncle while he lived there—something I will always regret.

I didn't know I would receive only one more letter from him. He wrote it on October 12, 1989, the same day his POW medal arrived at his house in California. But he would never know that his medal had been delivered.

Five days later on Tuesday, October 17, a massive earthquake struck the San Francisco Bay Area. I tried to call my cousin Lee in Haywood but all lines were down. The next morning, I called Weldon in Mexico. He had spent the previous night and the morning before my call frantically telephoning his family members. He sounded calm but strained as he told me he had learned they were all unhurt although some had experienced substantial loss of property. It was clear to me he regretted being so distant from them.

That night he suffered a fatal heart attack. I don't remember who called to tell me the sad news—if it was Lee or my grandmother—but the news put me in a state of shock. Weldon's death seemed so unreal. He had stayed with my family only a few weeks before and had been full of life then. In my mind I replayed again and again my final phone conversation with him. He knew everyone in California was OK—he was the one who told me that so I no longer attempted to call California to check on my cousins.

I replayed his recent visit to my family. I recalled that his visit did have an air of finality about it—he was intent on seeing my son who had moved out and Weldon seemed to seize every moment we were together. Did he know he did not have long to live? Or having experienced being a POW and recently reliving that experience, was he seizing every moment knowing that life, no matter how long, was too short?

Grandmother and I discussed his last visit with her in Lubbock. She too had the feeling that he knew his time was short.

Lee flew to Mexico to retrieve Weldon's body. I did not attend the funeral because of the earthquake damage at the airport and surrounding roads. I wrote his family a letter expressing my profound sense of loss.

Lee wrote back: "Cindy, thanks very much for your letter to the family—I read it before we all went to Dad's funeral. Thanks also for writing so much to Dad. You meant a *lot* to him!! Thanks also for motivating Dad to write about his war experience. We're all fine. Please give our love to your family when you see them. Love, Lee."

And Weldon's POW medal? When it arrived in California on October 12, his family didn't tell him. They planned to surprise him with it on his 65th birthday when Weldon was to be in California to see them all. Weldon died 22 days before his 65th birthday.

With the confidence of knowing that the talent ran in my family, I went on to realize my dream of becoming a published writer and to become an active participant in the space program.

And with this book, Weldon too, realizes his dream of becoming a writer.

APPENDIX—Why I Support the POW Medal
from an editorial and speech
by Cynthia Price, May 1991

The Gulf War is over. Just last week, the remainder of our active military troops began their long-awaited journey home. Perhaps the largest collective sigh of relief in this country came when Iraq released our prisoners of war.

Remember those images of POWs aired by Iraqi television a few short months ago? Haunting visions of battered faces, bowed heads, and stilted, monotone statements emitted from our TVs. Fears for their safety and well-being coursed through our hearts. Particular concern and focus centered around the fate of a young American woman, 21-year-old Army Specialist Melissa Rathburn-Nealy.

But now they are all safe and home. In March, the former Army POWs were awarded National Defense Service medals, Purple Hearts for those who were injured, and Prisoner of War Medals.

The POW Medal is a fairly new award—established by the Defense Department in 1985 as a token of a grateful nation for those who were U.S. prisoners of war in World War I, World War II, Korea, or Vietnam. Immediately, the formation of the new medal was met with controversy. This controversy continues today.

The basic issue surrounding the POW Medal is: are POWs heroes? One dictionary defines heroism as "a feat of courage and nobility of purpose." Yet there are those who say that "surrender, even unavoidable surrender," is hardly a feat of courage or nobility of purpose. There are those who say we should save our hero worship and medals for "those who have taken risks, saved and protected the lives of others and put themselves in danger; in short, those who have acted, successfully or not, but not those who have just suffered, and this not by choice." [editorial entitled "Let's quit treating POWs like they were heroes," by Si Frumkin, *Houston Chronicle*, April 3, 1991]

Tell that to Everett Alvarez, Jr. Alvarez endured 8-1/2 years of imprisonment in the hell-hole dubbed the Hanoi Hilton. Those nightmare years covered periods of torture, sickness, and the aching loneliness of solitary confinement—all separated by periods of excruciating monotony. To combat the tiresome monotony and to boost each other's morale, Alvarez and his fellow POWs formed a speakers club. They challenged each other to give five-minute speeches with only 30 seconds to prepare. As you can imagine, most of those speeches were about family and home life—reminders that helped them to survive their ordeal as POWs. ["A Prisoner's Tale" condensed from *Chained Eagle* by Everett Alvarez, Jr. and Anthony S. Pitch, *Reader's Digest*, August 1990]

Here's another example of POWs as heroes. When journalist Charles Kuralt was in Moscow in 1985 covering a summit meeting, he was sought out by an elderly Russian man who had a story for him. The man had been a prisoner of war in Germany in World War II. Next to the Russian concentration camp was the American POW camp. The Americans received food from the Red Cross, but the Russians did not, and they were dying by the hundreds. The Americans began throwing parcels at night over the 10-foot fence that separated the camps. The old man estimated that over 9,000 pounds of food were freely given by the American POWs at the risk of their own lives. In gratitude, the old man memorized the names of those Americans, later wrote the names down and forty years later, read them to Charles Kuralt. Kuralt listened to those American names being recited in a Russian accent and he later wrote, "I knew I was hearing a roll call of heroes." ["The Russian Who Never Forgot" condensed from *A Life on the Road* by Charles Kuralt, *Reader's Digest*, November 1990.]

These are examples of heroism as feats of courage and nobility of purpose described as worthy of recognition and medals, yet which some claim POWs have not earned. They are not alone in their initial assessment of the POW Medal. My uncle Weldon Squyres became a prisoner of war in Germany during World War II when his B-24 was shot down during a bombing raid. A few years ago when I wrote and told him about the new POW Medal, his reply was: "The thought struck me as odd since there is nothing particularly heroic about being taken prisoner...but maybe there is in surviving it." Those words spoken by a former POW to me contain justification for the POW Medal. Perhaps heroism lies in just surviving the experience of being a POW. Let me tell you about my uncle.

It was the second time he was shot down when my uncle became a prisoner of war. He and other crew members bailed out of their flaming Liberator aircraft, reluctantly leaving behind the bodies of their friends—fellow crew members who were unquestionably dead—killed in the ferocious attack by the German fighters. My uncle was quickly captured by the Germans and crowded with other prisoners like cattle into boxcars to be transported for endless miserable days to the stalags. After interrogations, his life settled into a cold, hungry, pitiful existence. At one point, he traded his high school ring to a guard for a can of sugar. Another time, a pack of cigarettes for sausage and cheese which were shared with other fellow prisoners. There were forced marches through rain, frozen sleet and snow. Rumors of mass killings of American prisoners made him and two other POWs plan a desperate escape into, of all places, a German POW camp housing British soldiers, where they all were later rescued by General Montgomery's forces.

Are POWs heroes? Yes. Do they deserve their own medal? Absolutely. The POW Medal is a symbol of a grateful nation and an appreciative people for POWs, all of whom had their lives at risk. The medal also serves a recognition of the ordeal they went through as prisoners of war. Let's not cheapen the homecoming of our recent POWs by insisting that they were not heroes. More importantly, let's hope and pray there are no more POWs.

About the Author

Cynthia Price was born Cynthia Anne Squyres on an Air Force base in Illinois and raised across the United States. She has made Texas her home for the past few decades.

In 1971, in response to a dare, she auditioned and landed a position as a news and weather anchor for a small television station outside Houston, Texas. At the same time, reporter Jessica Savitch was making the news at Channel 11 in Houston. In her short-lived television career, Cynthia was occasionally mistaken for Ms. Savitch, who went on to anchor national news at a major network in Washington, DC before her death. Cynthia contributed her experiences as a pioneering newswoman in the shadow of Jessica Savitch to *Golden Girl*, the best-selling biography of Savitch by Alanna Nash.

Cynthia's professional writing career began when she was employed at an advertising agency in the mid-70s. There she was mentored by a photojournalist who had had works published in *Time* magazine and other national publications. Today she credits the ad agency's grueling schedule of writing promotional copy and press releases about uninteresting subjects within tight deadlines as training her to be a disciplined writer. At the same time she began to freelance. One of her first published articles was an interview with singer/actor John Denver.

In 1982, Cynthia's attention was directed to the space program. That year a Texas company launched the first privately-funded rocket from Matagorda Island. When a Kansas newspaper decried the private launch calling for "a ban on private rocketry" and to "leave rocket launches to the government," Cynthia responded with what would become the first of many editorials and articles about space.

Later she was employed as a copywriter and public relations coordinator at a Houston advertising agency that served aerospace and other high-tech clients. During this time, she broadened her knowledge about the unique space industry. She also managed the press coordination and public relations for the annual presentation of the National Space Trophy.

Her interest and knowledge of space exploration led to employment with the largest aerospace contractor for NASA's Space Station Freedom program. There she served as a technical writer/ editor and as a research analyst. She also formed the space advocacy group, the Space Station Freedom Fighters, which delivered over 40,000 signatures to the White House in support of NASA's space station program.

In 1993, she formed her own research and writing firm, Space Research Associates. After the launch of the first U.S. component to the International Space Station in 1998, Cynthia announced her "retirement" from space station advocacy to devote her resources to writing and private space ventures. Cynthia continues writing about space, nature, boating, travel, business, gerontology, and other general interest topics. She has been published in over 50 journals and periodicals, and was the senior editor of *Orbiter* magazine. She has also served as a medical test subject for NASA, flying in the astronaut training aircraft KC-135, otherwise known as the "Vomit Comet."

Today Cynthia is a noted columnist and speaker. She lives in League City, Texas, with husband Marty, an assortment of cats and fish, and an iguana named Lucy.

She still hopes to fly into space.